# WHAT'S BEHIND OUT-OF-CONTROL US HEALTH CARE SPENDING?

# WHAT'S BEHIND OUT-OF-CONTROL US HEALTH CARE SPENDING?

The Evolution of U.S. Health Care Spending Post World War II

DR. EDGAR A. PEDEN

Copyright © 2014 by Dr. Edgar A. Peden.

Library of Congress Control Number: 2014913331
ISBN: Hardcover 978-1-4990-4391-4
Softcover 978-1-4990-4392-1
eBook 978-1-4990-4390-7

All rights reserved. No part of this book may be reproduced or transmitted in any form or by any means, electronic or mechanical, including photocopying, recording, or by any information storage and retrieval system, without permission in writing from the copyright owner.

Any people depicted in stock imagery provided by Thinkstock are models, and such images are being used for illustrative purposes only. Certain stock imagery © Thinkstock.

This book was printed in the United States of America.

Rev. date: 10/24/2014

**To order additional copies of this book, contact:**
Xlibris
1-888-795-4274
www.Xlibris.com
Orders@Xlibris.com
649644

# CONTENTS

Acknowledgements ............................................................... 9

1. Introduction .................................................................. 11

2. Relative health care spending history (a quantitative look) ..... 23

3. Modeling relative health care spending growth ..................... 35

4. Empirical results ............................................................. 53

5. Conclusion .................................................................... 67

Appendix ........................................................................... 79

Biographies ....................................................................... 85

References ........................................................................ 87

# What's behind out-of-control US health care spending?

## The Evolution of U.S. Health Care Spending

### Post World War II

An Empirical Analysis: 1948—2009

### by Edgar A. Peden

### assisted by Mark S. Freeland[1]

*A [rule] trajectory is the process by which a novel rule is originated, adopted, and retained in a carrier population, such that it eventually becomes coordinated in the economic system resulting in a new economic order.*

-Kurt Dopfer and Jason Potts, *The General Theory of Economic Evolution, p 12* (2008)

**ABSTRACT:** *Post-World War II U.S. government data (1948-2009) show that the health care spending percentage of consumption (relative health spending) rose from 5.3 to 20.9 percent, starting after the permanent extension of the (initially war-related) tax exclusion of the employer costs of employee health insurance. The rule change, abetted by a rise in real income, has been highly correlated with the ensuing rise in coverage demand (1) by firms without coverage competing*

---

[1] Edgar A. Peden is an independent health policy consultant and researcher based in Frederick, Maryland. Mark S. Freeland is an economist in the Office of the Actuary at the Centers for Medicare and Medicaid Services (CMS). The statements expressed in this article are those of the author and do not necessarily reflect the views of CMS. **Keywords:** Evolutionary Economics, Complexity, Adaptation, Autocatalytic Feedback, Rule, Health Care Spending, Meso-Macro, Trajectory. Comments to rhohat@comcast.net. **JEL Classification: B0, C5, E21, H2, I11, K34, N32**

*for employees and (2) by employees seeking to expand what was covered. These two factors raised coverage levels and increased the demand for health care and subsequently increased both relative health spending and relative medical prices. An autocatalytic (i.e., self-generating) feedback pattern emerged whereby these two factors led to further increases in coverage demand, which in turn led to growth in these two factors once again. This inter-temporal process followed a trajectory closely approximated by the logistic diffusion growth model equation, which this study estimates using the above-noted government data. The rising prices of medical care eventually resulted in appeals for government coverage for those without access to employer insurance, inducing the U. S. government in 1966 to provide coverage for the elderly (through Medicare) and the poor (Medicaid); other coverage (e.g., for the disabled) was added later. Adding government coverage appears to have accelerated demand still more, raising both relative spending and prices. The autocatalytic pattern continued until the early 1990s when managed care instituted by insurance companies and government regulation constrained relative health care spending to about 17 percent from 1991 to 2000. However, rising coverage levels were undoubtedly what caused this percentage to grow once again from 2000 to 2009 in spite of continuing—and even increased—rules and government regulations. My econometric estimates are consistent with an emergent complex self-organizing health care market, characterized historically by the above noted logistic diffusion equation. Relative health care spending and prices were still rising as of 2009, suggesting that further coverage expansion, such as the Affordable Care Act of 2010, would accelerate both relative spending and price growth yet again.*

# Acknowledgements

The first person I want to thank is Elizabeth Stallman-Brown, my editor. Her expertise and help in preparing the manuscript has been invaluable. Her patience and kindness has made her a joy to work with. The assistance I received from my good friend and colleague Mark Freeland (from the Center of Medicare and Medicaid Services, Office of the Actuary) has been a great help in putting this book together, starting from the time two decades ago that he first proposed doing the precursor to the current work. Cathy Cowan, Mark's co-worker, has provided me with the data I needed in a timely, professional, and pleasant manner, even as I sought to update it each year or asked her for supplementary data.

Finally, I want to thank my loving wife, Kathryn Groth, who shared the trials and stresses of this study. Her comments (even though her expertise lies elsewhere) proved to be valuable to me in all I did.

## 1. Introduction

*There are three kinds of lies: lies, damn lies, and statistics.*

*-Popularized by Mark Twain (originated by Leonard H. Courtney, 1895)*

Counter to what Mr. Twain might have advised, this study's going to do it again; that is, develop a hypothesis, and then—using statistics—test it with government data (and we all know they don't lie, don't we?).

This study updates 1995 and 1998 analyses of post-World War II (WWII) National Health Expenditure (NHE) data.[i] The previous studies used a standard neoclassical model. The current study covers additional years through 2009, adds managed care and government regulatory effects, and uses an evolutionary economic model of a health care sector characterized by complexity and emergent properties. My central purpose here is to explore, from an evolutionary perspective, the drivers of the persistent growth in relative health spending. In particular, why do we all pay such a large and growing portion of our income for health care "and yet, in many cases, not receive the health services we need?

This study agrees with the two previous findings (by myself and Mark Freeland) that relative health spending growth has been induced by increasing insurance coverage levels. All three studies agree that the root of the growth in relative health spending was a single rule change, *the post-war extension of the employer tax exclusion for employment-related health care insurance.* However, the current model puts the results into a self-organizing historical evolutionary paradigm that allows for "the structural uncertainty inherent in [the] evolutionary process [of a complex autocatalytic feedback system]."[ii] This paradigm is structured around dynamic trajectories that that can be affected by various factors. In contrast the standard neoclassical model espouses a static view, using comparative statics to analyze the movement from one equilibrium to another.

This story is not a simple tale of rising costs; instead I must account for a multiplicity of factors. At the end of the study, I hope to present a better picture of the historical events that induced relative health spending to grow so precipitously. A note of caution is in order: with an evolutionary-economic approach, one would not expect to find or demonstrate some universal principle; instead one typically finds dynamic behaviors and tendencies that might be expected to recur under circumstances that mimic those of the past. The health care sector is a complex evolutionary system, much like a dynamic biological system; it changes over time and is irreversible. As Stuart Kauffman relates, "At levels of complexity above atoms, the universe is on a pathway, or trajectory, that will never repeat."[iii] This contrasts with time-reversible systems such as Newton's laws and neoclassical economics. But discovering lessons from what has occurred will enable the formulation of a few historical lessons that may be applicable in designing future policies.

**Economics as an evolutionary science.** Increasingly, economists are employing an evolutionary perspective to understand and predict economic phenomena. And that is what I do here. So what is it and how does it work? Eric Beinhocker tells us that:

> Evolution is an *algorithm*: it is an all-purpose formula for innovation, a formula that, through its special brand of trial and error, creates new designs and solves difficult problems. Evolution can perform its tricks not just in the "substrate" of DNA, but in any system that has the right information-processing and information-storage characteristics . . . In short, evolution's [recipe is simple,] "differentiate, select, and amplify . . ."[iv]

From an economic perspective, evolution is the source of "novelty, knowledge, and growth."[v]

Beinhocker goes on to say that " . . . both economic and biological systems are subclasses of a more general and universal class of evolutionary systems . . ." that researchers believe follow "general laws of evolutionary systems."[iv] Thus "[i]f the economy is truly an evolutionary system . . ." it will follow those general laws. Beinhocker also states that these laws of economics do not "imply that we will ever be able to make perfect predictions about the economy, but [they do] imply that we might someday have a far deeper understanding of economic phenomena than we do today."[vii]

To distinguish biological and social scientific evolution, I note that economics follows rules of operation found in the book *The General Theory of Economic Evolution*, by Kurt Dopfer and Jason Potts (D&P).[viii]

The evolutionary ontology of the social science 'economics' is made up of ideas expressed as *generic rules*, which relate to operations on resources; D&P distinguish these from biological rules, which are *genetic*. Whereas "[g]enetic rules replicate biologically, generic rules 'are communicated' socially." In evolutionary economics the generic rules that evolve can be the cognitive and behavioral rules of the individual, the coordination of people with social rules, or the organization of matter and/or energy with technical rules. But all of these rules need to fit together; thus economic evolution—like biological evolution—includes not only changes in its generic rules, but also the ongoing process of their coordination.[ix]

**Health care as a complex adaptive system.** Economics in the traditional neoclassical framework is essentially static, characterized by equilibrium in all markets and across all markets in what is known as general equilibrium. When there are shocks from changes in technology, public policy, consumer preferences, or any of the myriad other factors affecting markets, market changes will occur over time, but from one static equilibrium to another. By contrast, following Stuart Kauffman, " . . . a complex system is a system of many dynamically interacting parts or particles. In such systems the micro-level interactions of the parts or particles lead to the emergence of macro-level patterns of behavior." As an example, he tells us that a single isolated water molecule is a rather humdrum phenomenon, but if one puts "a few billion water molecules together and adds some energy in the right way, one gets the complex macro pattern of a whirlpool . . . , [which] is the result of the dynamic interactions between the individual molecules." The whirlpool is an 'emergent' property of these interactions. In the same way, economies are groups of people who collectively interact to develop and adapt their behaviors in complex emergent patterns that process information and systematized the economy as a whole.[x]

Although a formal definition of "complexity" has proved elusive, Scott E. Page tells us that a "system can be considered complex if its agents meet four qualifications: diversity, connection, interdependence, and adaptation."[xi] I would add that a complex system will have "strong interactions among its elements," and that what happens in the system now can strongly influence the probabilities of many kinds of later occurrences.[xii]

Clearly, something other than the standard neoclassical approach is required. As Mark Blaug says, "health economics is a field which must make the average neoclassical [economist] squirm because it challenges his or her standard assumptions at every turn."[xiii] Given the multiplicity of reasons to steer away from a neoclassical framework, including my own inclinations, I proceed to analyze health care as a complex adaptive system with emergent properties.

My intention is to treat the health care market as an evolutionary complex system with emergent properties that can be analyzed using post-WWII data. In doing this, however, it is also necessary to incorporate the unique features of the health care sector. Hodgson tells us that "while *health* itself is a universal need, needs for *health care* are largely involuntary, varied, and idiosyncratic." He adds that "[t]hese issues have important consequences for the planning of health care systems . . . ." Combining the inherent dynamism of complex adaptive systems generally, with these unique properties of modern health care, as well as its needs and capabilities, results in "an opening for alternative approaches to health care economics . . . [whose systems he concludes] . . . are non-linear, complex, and have strong interactive effects."[xiv]

**Micro-meso-macro.** Until recently, neoclassical economists have been used to thinking of economic analysis as taking place at either the micro or macro, the former referring to the individual and interactive behavior of consumers and firms, and the latter to—economy-wide economic behavior—a sum-total of the former. However, Dopfer, Foster, and Potts (DFP) tell us that "From the evolutionary perspective, one cannot directly sum micro into macro."[xv] In this study, the health care sub-sector analyzed—and where given rules and norms apply within this subsector—is only part of the macro economy; thus the proper reference for the sub-sector is "meso." This is apparent in context as follows.

> o Micro structure refers to individual rule carriers, as well as the systems they organize. Their inter-relationships and behaviors are complex. Micro structure occurs within the elements of the meso and macro structures, and includes their rules for both individual agents and the systems they organize. Together, these factors provide the basis for an ontologically coherent framework for an analysis of economic evolution as changes in the micro domain, and thus within the meso and macro domains as well.

> o Meso structure consists of a rule and its population of actualizations, which can be thought of as a macro-economic sub-sector and is thus subject to macro-level rules. For the health care meso-sector, emergent properties from macro-level rules and the interacting micro behaviors of the consuming and service units (carrying their own health care rules) result in the emergent aggregate behaviors that constitute the meso market. Within this scenario, DFP posit a

"meso trajectory," [xvi] as a way of understanding the micro-processes, as well as the meso, and ultimately the macro consequences involved.

o Macro structure is the emergent behavior of interacting meso sub-sectors.

While emergent micro behavior results in meso and macro behavior, this does not mean that either is predictable from micro behavior or that macro behavior is predictable from meso behavior. As Stuart Kauffman tells us in his book, *Reinventing the Sacred*, " . . . [while] the economy is ceaselessly creative, [it is] beyond the reach of reductionism . . . 2"[xvii] By contrast, reductionism is a key feature of the neoclassical economic model.

**Health care as a meso-macro system with emergent properties.** The health care sector is a diverse, agent-connected, interdependent, and adaptive. But in addition, it is also a meso market within the macro-economy. In particular, health care spending is a subset of consumption, and this study examines the portion of consumption going toward health care, which is thus meso-macro, and is defined as *relative health care spending*. Its trajectory is the subject of the following analysis. Emergent properties of relative health care spending may or may not follow from the micro behaviors of the agents, but often, what occurs at the higher levels of analysis, differs from the micro level, not just in scale, but in kind.[xviii] In sum, I analyze emergent relative health care spending historically as a complex adaptive system in an evolutionary framework.

Rule changes can have a large impact on emergent properties, which themselves can have subsequent effects on the further

---

[2] From Kauffman, p 3, "Reductionism, in its strongest form holds that all the rest of reality, from organisms to a couple in love on the banks of the Seine, is ultimately nothing but particles or strings in motion. [And that] . . . the explanations for higher-order entities are to be found in lower order entities."

evolution of a system. It is this study's purpose to examine the historical evolution of the health care sector from an initial rule change (and later reactive modifications) that resulted in its historical and current path. Emergent behaviors often take place over a long period of time and, as found in Aziz-Alaoui and Bertelle, "cause and effect need not be close in time."[xix]

**Relative health care spending: A brief historical overview.** In 1942 the US government began granting employers tax exclusions for employee health care insurance purchases to allow wage increases without violating war-related wage controls.[xx] The controls ended with the war, but the tax exclusions were explicitly continued after 1945. Subsequently, employer sponsored health care insurance started to spread, though not all companies purchased it. Relative health care spending began to rise, as did relative medical prices—i.e. the medical price index divided by price index of total consumption.[3] The differential financial advantage of selling medical services over other consumption induced by added coverage resulted in demand by both employers and employees to add to or expand coverage still more. Thus the financial advantage was seen in both the growth of relative health care spending and the growth in relative medical prices. For firms, the addition or expansion of coverage became a way to compete for employees. A feedback mechanism arose, whereby greater coverage increased the relative demand for health care which then resulted in higher relative medical prices and greater relative health care spending, which, in turn, further increased the demand for coverage. Over time, society came to see higher relative medical prices as unfair and punitive to those who didn't—or weren't able to—receive the subsidies inherent in the employer tax exclusion.[4]

---

[3] Relative spending on health care = quantity x relative price of health care. In our case, the latter is the personal consumption index for medical care divided by the personal consumption index for all goods and services.

[4] Here fairness is a societal norm, or unwritten rule.

To ease the effects of this perceived unfairness, the elderly and poor were provided with Medicare and Medicaid, respectively, starting in 1966. The creation of these programs was followed by the creation of numerous similar public programs (e.g., the disabled were added to Medicare in 1973). But the more additional subsidies became available, the more health care demand rose vis-à-vis overall consumption demand,—and the stronger the stimulus became,—both to relative medical prices and relative health care spending.[5]

As seen above, continuing coverage increases (inherent in the tax exclusion and the new government insurance programs) brought about an increased demand for medical services seen in the higher relative medical prices and additional funding. But on a positive note, it also resulted in a continuously rising derived demand for both existing and new services of medical providers, medical firms, insurance companies and research institutions; and many of these services included technical innovations and organizational improvements. At the same time, the products of medical firms were similarly improved. Because innovations are constantly occurring across all sectors of the economy, many probably would have come about in any case, but others occurred because of the increased stimulus. In yet other cases, the increases in demand—seen in both the market for products and services and for those producing them—simply raised relative medical prices and input costs, as will be seen below in the case of tonsillectomies. In spite of these complications, there is no doubt that medical services and products have been greatly enhanced in both their quantity and quality because of the demand-induced medical innovations.

**Managed Care.** As insurance companies became aware of the effects of rising coverage, a number of other countervailing emergent properties manifested themselves. In particular, with the passage of 'The Health Maintenance Organization [HMO] Act' passed by Congress in 1973, managed care became

---

[5] Here these two concepts are meso-macro concepts by definition (as seen above).

available for the management of an individual's health care in exchange for an overall payment. In addition, fee-for-service insurance companies started adopting many of the managed care innovations by providing a designated comprehensive market basket of medical services under various payment options and copay arrangements. An emergent property of managed care, whether HMOs or fee-for-service packages, has been the advent of managed care insurers hiring or contracting with providers to provide care at prices lower than those typically found on a strictly fee-for-service basis—often with fewer or curtailed services—in exchange for guaranteeing them clientele. Packages of medical services also brought—in addition to the tax incentive to purchase insurance—broader coverage (e.g., dental, vision, and hearing defect coverage). Added also was the often contentious process of having to justify individual and provider claims to both private and public insurers, with sometimes tedious legal steps involved. Patient claims became subject to review and, in many cases, have been denied. Provider practices were monitored and subject to stringent regulation by the federal government. In any case, what had been a rather straightforward market involving patients and providers before the end of WW II, evolved to include large insurance companies, lawyers, practice managers, numerous claims representatives, and lobbyists (for vested interests) as well as an enlarged bureaucracy to handle claims, enforce rules, and process the paper work supporting these increased activities. As a result, receiving and giving health care services has become one of the most complicated and arduous fiscal activities facing many Americans and their health care providers. Today, buying health care is not as easy or straightforward as buying other goods and services.

Government health care programs followed the private market with managed care programs of their own; they added fee-for-service regulations, emulating what the private market was doing. With its increased involvement in the health care sector, the federal government also increased its regulatory activity, not only for its own programs, but also for private sector medical care.

While managed care was instituted in 1973, it took a while for it to have a fiscal impact on relative health care insurance spending and its growth. Indeed, it was not until the 1990s that it had a significant effect on relative health care spending growth. As seen from the data below, managed care and additional government regulation resulted in a temporary hiatus in relative health spending growth during the 1990s, but a markedly smaller effect on relative medical price growth.

Government regulations became more prevalent in the health care sector. However, these regulations also resulted in greater transaction costs throughout the sector—for patients, providers, suppliers of medical equipment, pharmaceutical firms, and even the government itself. For example, one doctor, who started his practice with a single nurse/office assistant, now has seven employees, mainly to handle insurance matters of all stripes.[xxi]

**Two general notes.** (1) Many medical advances came about because of on-going increases in insurance coverage throughout my 60-year data period, increasing the intensity of services, but having an even greater effect on relative price growth: before, during, and after managed care was phased in (as shown in Table 1). (2) As we shall see, many of the phenomena in the historical evolution of the health care sector—such as the increasing demand for health care insurance induced by the tax break—follow from basic economic logic: all else being equal, people will pay less out-of-pocket for insured services, and consume more. Other emergent phenomena might not have been foreseen when the original rule was put in place, such as the rise of HMOs and managed care, the increased role of government, and the rise in bureaucratic complexity made necessary by changes in the increasingly insurance-based regulatory system.

**Does health care insurance increase welfare?** In the 1940s and 50s Milton Friedman showed that people and firms who voluntary buy any type of insurance (e.g. health care, life, home, or automobile) enhance their personal welfare by insuring against future catastrophic threats to their income or welfare.[xxii] But this is may no longer be completely the case for health care insurance, as government tax exclusions and other subsidies have resulted in the incentive to over-insure; coverage is often used for routine expenses (such as an office visit for an inoculation or a prescription for an antibiotic to treat a minor throat infection) unrelated to significant income loss, disability, or death, making its overall welfare effects unclear.[6]

---

[6] As shown in the Appendix, results from our previous work, increases in income were also instrumental in increasing the demand for insurance. Public insurance for individuals also abetted this process, but the latter undoubtedly occurred because relative medical price increases disadvantaged certain groups, e.g. the elderly, the poor, and others; most recently uncovered children.

## 2. Relative health care spending history (a quantitative look)

**Relative health care spending and insurance.** Up until the end of WWII health care spending had been a stable percentage of consumption. The Bureau of Economic Analysis (BEA) measure of health care spending averaged 3.5 percent of consumption for 1929-1934, 3.4 percent for 1935-1940, and 3.3 percent for 1941-1946.[xxiii,7] In 1942, the US government began granting employers tax exclusions for employee health care insurance purchases to allow wage increases without violating war-related wage controls.[xxiv] The controls ended with the war, but the tax exclusions were explicitly continued after 1945. This continuation was, in effect, a huge rule change, which amounted to an evolutionary *punctuated equilibrium* that, in the words of D&P, resulted "in a new economic order" for health care and health care spending. As related by Paul Krugman, "what is necessary to create [an economic] punctuated equilibrium is for some processes to proceed much faster than others . . . ."[xxv] And that's what happened in the US health care market. In effect, stable relative health spending from 1929 through 1946 gave way to dramatic—and long-lasting—growth that fed upon itself; growth that was,

---

[7] It appears that prior to 1929, relative health spending was as low or lower than it became subsequently. Another caution is that it is necessary to be very cautious in using old data, since it cannot be compared to what we now have available, for example, in the National Health Expenditure Accounts. But it is suggestive. In one large "U.S. Commission of Labor" Study by Carroll Wright for 1891 (Fifth and Sixth Annual Report), survey of industrial workers . . . reports "sickness and death expenses" by family turns out to be 3-5 % of total expenses." Employment data from the U.S. Department of Census indicate that in 1930 the percentage of employed civilians in health occupations was 1.8 percent of the total, somewhat above the 1.2, 1.3, and 1.5 percent respectively, for 1900, 1910, and 1920, as found in TE Getzen <u>Health Economics and Financing</u>, 3rd ed. J. Wiley & Sons 2007 Table 13.3, "U.S. Health Employment 1850-2000", page 322. From this (admittedly partial data) we might surmise that the health care spending percentage of consumption would have been lower prior to 1929 than it was from 1929-46.

according to Robert Ulanowicz, "*autocatalytic.*"[xxvi] The *relative* health care spending portion of overall consumption grew an average of 2.3 percent per year over the 62-year period 1948-2009, cumulatively 292 percent from 5.3 percent in 1948 to 20.9 percent in 2009.

As seen above, the initial result of the continuation of the tax exclusion was a rise in demand for employer coverage by uninsured employees and by nonparticipating employers competing for labor. Because of the autocatalytic feed-back effect, subsequent coverage expansions increased health care demand vis-a-vis other consumption still further, and thus increased relative health care spending further. Medical prices rose relative to other prices, which further disadvantaged uninsured employees, those not employed, and employers forced to compete for labor (but not offering coverage). This created pressures for additional employment-related coverage. The inter-temporal result of continuing employer exclusions increases perpetuated the autocatalytic feedback loop: increased coverage, higher relative health care spending and prices, more coverage, higher relative spending and prices, and so on. This feedback loop made medical care ever more costly and further disadvantaged those without coverage, most particularly those not connected to the labor market.[8]

In 1966, when the government expanded its own insurance coverage to include Medicare (for the elderly) and Medicaid (for the poor)[9], health care demand was given further impetus, accelerating both relative health care spending and relative medical prices. Between 1966 and 1971 relative health spending grew 25 percent and medical inflation exceeded all

---

[8] As we will see below, other factors (such as income growth) were also important determinants of relative health spending growth.

[9] The disabled were added to Medicare starting on the first day of fiscal 1974.

consumer inflation by 2 percent per year.[10] Extending this a bit further, from 1965 through 1975, relative health care spending grew 40 percent, from 7.8 to 10.9 percent of consumption (3.3 percent per year, about half of which was the result of higher relative medical prices).[11] Government expansion thus augmented the long-term autocatalytic pattern initiated by the original rule change, advantaging some while further disadvantaging those still not insured.

Subsequently, both private insurers and government continued to expand coverage, the latter often mandating more private employer coverage, adding more programs, and covering more services within existing programs. This has created a situation in which many individuals—such as those working for small employers that are less able to afford employee coverage—still lack employer coverage and do not qualify for government programs.[12] Often uninsured individuals access care only through hospital emergency rooms, where the law mandates care for everyone.

In the early 1990s (reacting to out-of-control health care spending) most fee-for-service insurance plans used their

---

[10] Although, as seen below, the Personal Consumption Price Index for health care is subject to some controversy.

[11] For a short period of time (1973-1974) the relative medical price index actually decreased as a result of the wage and price controls existing at that time. With these controls, and because of the increased demand for medical care created by the new government programs, relative real per capita consumption of medical care actually increased faster than relative medical prices, one of the only times in the 62-year data period that this occurred.

[12] States do not uniformly mandate employee coverage. Moreover, mandated coverage often applies only to employees working more than a certain number of hours per week (e.g. 30); thus the staff of some employers consists mostly of part-timers. Other employers avoid paying for health insurance by contracting out services to individuals who sell them their services or firms either not providing coverage or offering coverage of their own, which may or may not be inferior to that of the firm buying their services.

monopsony power to put managed care payment practices in place. The US government restrained health care spending growth by limiting payments for some of the services covered under its own programs and by restricting what was paid for. For example, beginning in 1983, hospital facility payments were based on diagnostic related groups rather the number of days stayed and ancillary services. In addition, the US government added managed care programs of its own. These measures, combined with other public-private restraints, caused 1991-2000 health care spending growth to be nearly equal to all consumption growth so that relative health care spending was unchanged for a decade at about 17 percent of consumption. Since relative medical prices continued to increase an average of 1.4 percent per year during this time,[xxvii] real relative health care spending (reflecting the quantity of services provided) was falling by a similar percentage. Indeed, both private and public care regulation restrained where health care services could be received and limited payouts to approved amounts to accredited providers for approved care. Many insurance claims were denied, some on questionable grounds, which led to increased litigation. These regulatory practices have continued, —and they still restrain health care spending growth. However, by the early 2000s increased coverage, along with lower unemployment, again caused health care spending growth to exceed consumption growth by substantial amounts.

From 2000 to 2009 relative health care spending grew 2.3 percent per year, with large growth rates in 2000-2003 and 2006-2009. The data for 1948-2009 show that the relative health care spending—which reached nearly 21 percent in 2009—was still growing at the end of the period.[xxviii]

Graph 1 shows relative health care spending for 1948-2009.

## Graph 1

## Health Care Spending as a Proportion of Consumption (1948-2009)

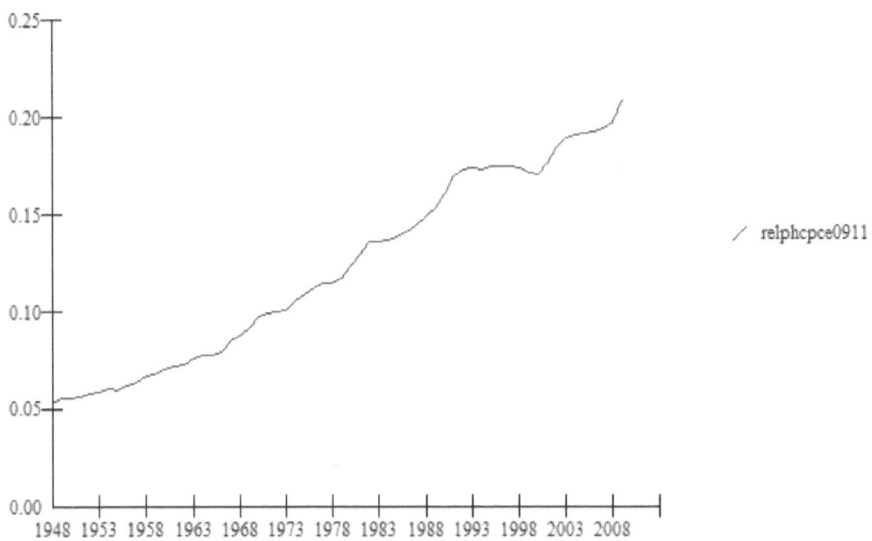

Graph 2 shows relative health care spending growth for 1948-2009.

The insured exercise leveraged purchasing power when buying health services—because each dollar out-of-pocket buys more than one dollar in services. For this reason,—supplying these services has been profitable, prompting disproportionately high investment in sophisticated technology and human capital. As shown in the next section, the result of increasing leverage has been continual increases in relative health care prices and quantities,—particularly the former,—with the latter growing slowly and intermittently, but generally positive.

## Graph 2

### Year-to-Year Growth in Health Care Spending as a Proportion of Consumption

### (1948 through 2009)

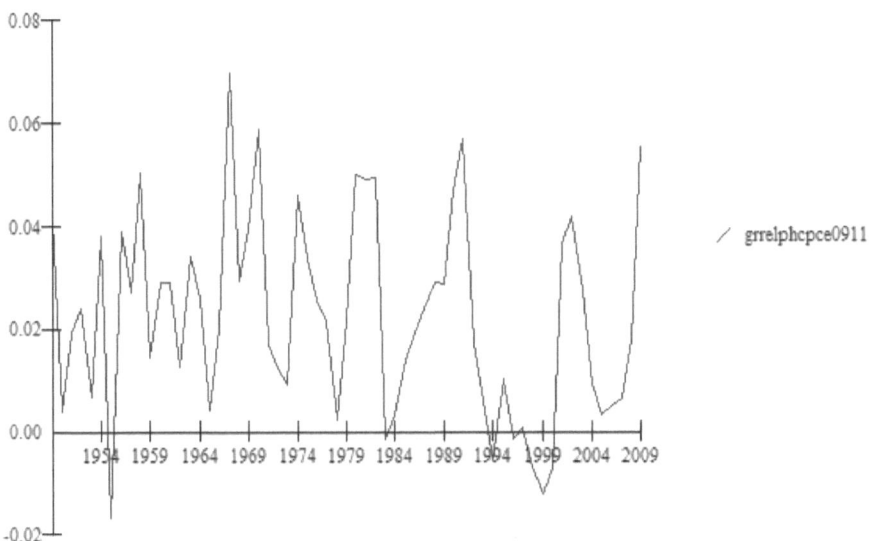

1948-2009 relative health care spending growth can be split into real and inflationary parts. To do so, three clarifications are necessary: First, the personal consumption of health care (PHC) comes from the National Health Expenditure Accounts (NHE), as reported by the Department of Health and Human Services, to include some services not included BEA's measure of the personal consumption of medical care. For instance Defense and Veterans' health spending, which were 3.5 percent of the total in 2009, are included in the former, but not the latter where they're classified as government spending. Second, one would expect the costs of these services—and their implicit prices—to follow closely what occurs in the health care sector as a whole because they compete in the same input markets (say for physicians) as the sector as a whole. Third, because the NHE data includes no price indexes, I assumed that the deflator for the personal consumption of medical care (PCE med) can be used to deflate PHC spending from the NHE data.[13, 14, xxix]

Using the BEAs PCE med (index) to deflate PHC spending, shows that the largest part of the 1948-2009 average relative health care spending growth of 2.26 percent per year was due to growth in relative prices (PCE med index/PCE overall index): 1.94 percent per year, versus 0.32 percent per year for relative real health spending growth. Cumulatively, real medical services grew 1.2 times as much as overall real consumption, while medical prices grew 3.2 times as much as consumer prices generally.[xxx] Table 1 gives a decade-by-decade look at how the components of relative health spending evolved over time.

**Tables**

---

[13] A number of economists have pointed out that government price indexes and sub-indexes (including the PCE medical deflator) do not accurately reflect actual price increases. See the ensuing endnote for details. This is the only place in this study where the PCE medical deflator is actually used, and here it is used for descriptive, not analytical purposes. For instance, the dependent variable I analyze is the year-to-year percentage changes in nominal consumption going for health care spending.

[14] Newhouse has criticized the use of the medical Consumer Price Index (medical CPI) in a 1992 article. Newhouse, Joseph P., "Medical Care Costs: How Much Welfare Loss?", The Journal of Economic Perspectives, Vol 6, No. 3 (Summer 1992): pp. 3-21. Part, but not all of the criticisms he makes apply to the medical personal consumption index (medical PCI). Others don't. Newhouse says that the medical (MCPI) measures input and not final goods and that would apply also to the medical PCE. He also says that the "Actual Prices of the medical CPI are not observed." But since the PCEs reflect transactions prices, this does not apply to the PCE for medical care. It is also true that neither index reflects quality changes. However, Newhouse's final criticism that the medical CPI weights out-of-pocket expenses, thus distorting the relative weights of the prices of services, does not apply to the PCEs which cover all services at their transaction prices.

## Table 1

### Parsing out the averages
### yearly percentage growth in relative health care spending

| Year-to-year average | Growth in the relative health care spending percentage of PCE | Growth in relative medical prices | Growth in relative real health care per capita Spending |
|---|---|---|---|
| 1948–1958 | 2.36 | 1.69 | 0.67 |
| 1958–1968 | 2.73 | 2.20 | 0.53 |
| 1968–1978 | 2.70 | 1.49 | 1.21 |
| 1978–1988 | 2.62 | 3.12 | -0.50 |
| 1988–1998 | 1.55 | 2.35 | -0.80 |
| 1998–2009 | 1.69 | 0.89 | 0.80 |
| 1948–2009 | 2.26 | 1.94 | 0.32 |

Table 1 shows that both relative prices and relative real per capita health care spending grew during the first three decades of my data (1948-1978), although the former grew faster than the latter. In the last three decades (1978-2009), relative real per capita health care actually showed a decline in real growth, as a result of negative growth in the two 1978-1998 decades, even as relative medical prices continued to grow. The last three-decade period reflects an increasing tendency to view growing relative health care spending as an economic problem, which led to increased managed care, both private and public. The growth in relative prices slowed across these three decades, first from 1978-1988 to 1988-1998, and then again in 1998-2009. This slowing undoubtedly occurred as a result of the exercise of insurers' monopsony power in purchasing services, even in the face of greater service intensity due to greater diagnostic testing and the greater availability of rigorous highly technical services such as chemotherapy and open heart surgery.

**Price index problems.** While a number of criticisms have been directed toward the weaknesses of the price indexes for health care (particularly the medical consumer price index),[xxxi] the PCE med index is subject to only some of these criticisms. In particular, the PCE med index measures, such as a day in the hospital, reflect input costs, which still might not reflect quality increases inherent in new technology. Yet unaccounted for quality changes are a criticism leveled at the indexes of most high-tech goods and services.[15] One could also argue that the large differences between relative medical price growth and relative real health care spending growth—comparing the first three decades of Table 1 to the last three—reflects actual changes in health care marketplace dynamics, based on managed care changes and increased government involvement, however imperfect the PCE med may be.[16],[xxxii] Finally, a number of *unchanged medical services*, for

---

[15] There has been much discussion over the years about whether price index increases might mask quality increases, not only in health care but also more broadly. In health care this is a particularly difficult area, as noted in the reference below.

[16] Price indexes are not always consistent across time, and so could result in measurement error in the statistics we cite. The BEA began using Producer Price Indexes (PPIs) instead of CPIs for different types of medical services. For example, the PPI for hospital care became available in Dec 1992 for levels and 1994 for annual percentage changes. The upshot is that beginning in the late 1990s BEA had better price indexes (with discounts taken out and greater controls for product changes), which they had to spice with CPIs for prior years. The data used are a potentially serious issue. If for instance, one looks at the BEA's definition of health care spending, one gets slightly higher growth in real health care spending than when deflating personal health care spending from the NHE accounts. Indeed this growth is about 0.33 percent higher in

example a tonsillectomy, have had price increases of at least twice the seven-fold increase in the overall PCE price index (1948-2009).[17]

In this study, I first present an algorithm reflecting the historical growth of relative health care spending in evolutionary terms—which results in an estimable equation. Second, I estimate the equation with time-series data (1948-2009) to track this growth.

---

the former, which is about twice what it is in the latter (1948—2009). However, in either case, price increases swamp real spending increases as the major determinant of relative health care spending growth.

[17] The tonsillectomy hospital price for 1948 is estimated by an actual bill for a tonsillectomy from 1946; for 2009 I requested prices for both inpatient and outpatient versions of the service from the CMS for Medicaid Services. When I say "at least seven times", I'm referring to the cheaper of the two for the latter year, the outpatient price.

## 3. Modeling relative health care spending growth

**Short run vs. long run.** John Foster noted that Alfred Marshall made a marked distinction between the short and long run. He tells us Marshall's *Principles of Economics* analyzed what occurs in the short run "and did not argue that price theory could be useful in understanding economic phenomena in a general sense, as has often been the case in post-Marshallian neoclassical economics . . . . [Indeed it is] an *approximation* for application in specific circumstances and over short time periods."[xxxiii] Marshall never produced the promised second long-run analysis. As Foster tells us,

> Post-Marshallian neoclassical economists, by arguing that the long-run general equilibrium price mechanism determines the course of the economic process in the long period and that quantity adjustments are short-run disequilibrium movements appropriate to the short-period, destroyed the attempts of both Marshall and Keynes to use comparative static analysis as a reasonable short-period approximation.[xxxiv]

However,

> . . . there is no need to dismantle Marshall's [short-run] price theory . . . in attempting to provide a coherent treatment of evolutionary [long-run] economics. What *is* necessary is to revive Marshall's agenda to provide an alternative theoretical approach that can offer a suitable approximation for scientific inquiry concerning evolutionary [long-run] change in the economic system . . . . [K]nowledge is acquired rather than imposed in the historical process of structuration. As such, knowledge itself constitutes structure that is complex and self-organized.[xxxv]

To understand long-run inter-temporal economic phenomena, I follow D&P in their general discussion of evolutionary economics.

As they point out, special economic concepts of knowledge already include preferences, markets, learning, technologies, human capital, and so on, as well as general-purpose technologies, contracts, laws, institutions, constitutions. As units of knowledge they are "the building blocks of wealth and the locus of evolutionary change . . . ," and are all based on rules. Indeed, "all economic knowledge and the growth of knowledge can be analyzed as a process of coordination and change in *rules*."[xxxvi]

Thus to analyze the health care market as a part of the economy for the 62-year period (1948-2009), I use an evolutionary model from Foster and Wild (F&W). [xxxvii] The initial rule change appears to have set this market on a long-run autocatalytic trajectory, which is the subject of my analysis. Previously, the history of health care spending has been analyzed (inappropriately, in my current view) using standard short-run neoclassical economic theory, where this former body of work includes my own past studies.[xxxviii]

**An evolutionary-economic model.** This study follows D&P's book, *The General Theory Of Economic Evolution*,[xxxix] in that I use their general evolutionary economic theory to characterize the history of the post-WW II health care spending as part of overall consumption (i.e. relative health care spending). D&P refer to a market as a *regime,* which they define as a cohesive part of the macro-economy with a carrier population participating in a market that is subject to rule changes (in law or custom) and a dynamic meso-macroeconomic trajectory affected by these changes. The econometric model I use is from F&W,[xl] adapted to analyze the trajectory of the relative health care spending subsequent to the initial rule change, while controlling for other factors. F&W estimate a long-run historic evolutionary trajectory as a complex adaptive system, unlike the standard models that are not time oriented. As D&P tell us, "[i]n neoclassical economics, the analogue of a trajectory is the path to equilibria . . . ." [xli] Here there are no equilibria; history matters.

**Why use an evolutionary approach?** To analyze the history of relative health care spending, evolutionary models are superior to neoclassical models for several reasons:

> o Health care is a path-dependent irreversible cumulative function of its history, which could have evolved differently. As an obvious example, medical advances are built upon if they succeed, or, like anything else, they are cut back or withdrawn if they fail or are superseded by further advances.
>
> o Since the initiating rule change, the healthcare regime has not tended toward a stable equilibrium, but has instead been characterized by continuous disequilibrium—a dynamic, changing growth process—not just because of exogenous factors, but also because of the endogenous dynamic self-organization of the regime itself. In particular, the regime has been subject to ongoing autocatalytic feedback effects.
>
> o Market participants—patients, providers, insurance plans, investors, and government—all make choices based on imperfect knowledge and the information available.
>
> o While prior analyses showed that coverage levels have had a highly significant stimulative effect on the growth of relative health care spending, the current evolutionary model provides an evolutionary rationale behind this *growth* as a non-linear function of insurance coverage *levels* and other factors. The F&W model allows for both short—and long-period causal factors, where the long-run factors endogenize "the fundamental parameters" to specify "a self-organization process."[xlii] To encompass both short—and long-run factors, I posit F&W's logistic diffusion equation as seen below.[xliii]
>
> o The neoclassical model was built around 19th century physics, with reversibility and equilibrium. My

evolutionary model is rooted in Marshall's biological approach, using Darwinian principles: irreversibility, non-equilibrium, and path dependence.

**Inter-temporal self-organization.** Because consumption has alternative uses other than health care, this study focuses on the meso-macro analytical concept, with health care spending (meso) as a percentage of total consumption (macro). In particular, it examines the dynamics of the relative health care spending trajectory; that is "the evolutionary path [after] a novel generic rule change, . . . ,"[xliv] in this case, the post-war exclusion of payments for employee health insurance from employer taxes.

Within the evolutionary paradigm, micro units can differ greatly in the choices they make in any given circumstance; but together these choices result in a discernible self-organization pattern at the meso-macro level, characterized by a spontaneous emergent aggregate trajectory over time.

Starting even before Adam Smith,[18] analysts had surmised that economies tend toward such spontaneous order. In the 20th century, Hayek couples the "twin ideas of evolution and spontaneous order,"[xlv] and Hodgson tells us that "[a system] can maintain [itself] . . . only if it evolve[s] the capacity to replicate or reproduce [its] structure." Like living animals and plants, such systems maintain an autonomy and continuity of pattern "despite the endless turnover of their constituents."[xlvi] Thus abstracting to relative health care spending growth should expedite our understanding of the emergent (meso-macro) economic patterns of relative health care spending. A reductionist perspective—with its micro unit interactions—would confound the analysis with too much detail. As anyone who has worked with individual-or firm-level data knows, randomness appears to occur at the micro level, with

---

[18] Adam Smith is usually considered to be the father of modern analytic economics, in part based on his book, *The Wealth of Nations*, published in 1776.

substantial variety in the structure and behavior of individual units".[xlvii] Given options, people will make a variety of choices. My purpose is not to denigrate micro-level analysis—the appropriateness of any particular level of analysis depends on the question examined—but to point out that a meso-macro level analysis is appropriate in this instance because of its emergent, self-organized structure building. Thus, this study's task is to specify how evolution and spontaneous order have manifested themselves in the inter-temporal dynamic process reflected in the path of relative health care spending.

**A model of innovation diffusion: The S-curve.**[xlviii] In the early days of any new innovation, there is a reluctance to adopt it and progress is slow. However, after a period during which positive experiences accumulate and various modifications are made, a profitable innovation suddenly takes off on an exponentially increasing curve. During this period, substantial investments are made in the new innovation and it increases exponentially. Beinhocker describes this process in terms of a new product or service innovation, where, each dollar invested in research and development (R&D) yields substantial gains in performance from the technology.[19] As expansion continues, acceleration slows and expansion becomes less and less on the margin, finally—in the long-run—reaching saturation, where marginal increases are zero. Graph 3 shows a hypothetical S-curve for this inter-temporal scenario.

---

[19] In this study I analyze the path of relative health care spending after the incentive modifying original employer tax exclusion rule changed and resulted in the trajectory that it ultimately followed.

## Graph 3

### After Innovation: Product's Percentage of the Market over Time

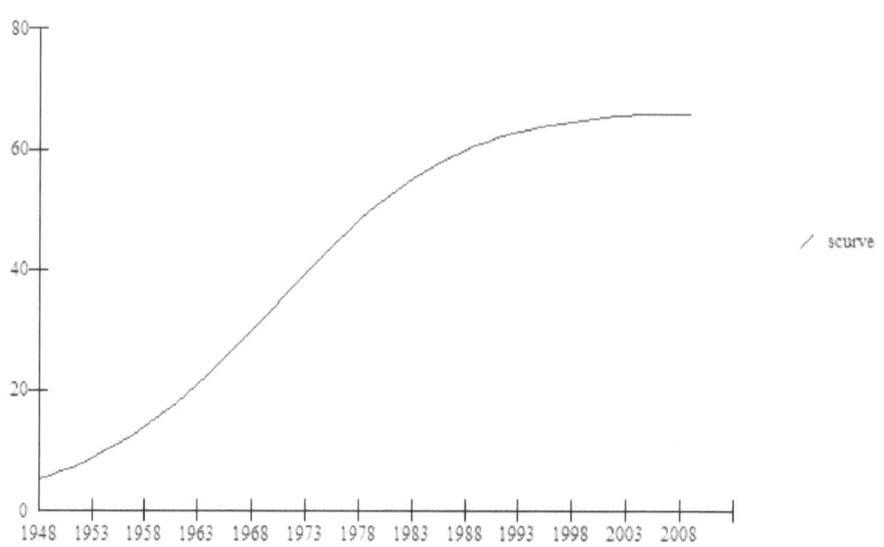

With a 62-year dynamic of new, improved services entering the health care market and a rejection of old ones, much more than a single innovation is involved. But one can adapt the F&W S-curve equation such that it applies to the (meso-macro) trajectory of relative health care spending itself.

**An S-curve of relative health care spending.** No one asks evolutionary biologists what species will evolve next. However, evolutionary economists find it necessary to evaluate what has gone on before in consistent ways that allow estimates of statistical value—not only to provide an analysis of what has transpired,—but also to project what might be expected in the future under a given set of circumstances.[xlix] For both purposes, I use an S-curve to track the trajectory of relative health care spending, such as that seen in Graph 3.

But why would relative health care spending evolve in this way? I address this question following an analogous F&W (meso-macro) analysis of "Building Society" deposits analysis, which examines the percentage these deposits make up of total Australian banking assets (the quantity of money, M4), where the Building Society deposits are a meso quantity and M4 is a macro quantity. The F&W S-curve of the percentage again has three phases over time, "with an underlying process of self-organization," resulting in their *self-organization logistic diffusion equation*. As would be the case with successful innovations generally, their first phase is *emergence*: a rule change in a sector creates a niche, in which innovations grow slowly at first and then accelerate. Their second phase is *inflexion*, in which "growth is approximately linear and structure-building becomes relatively routine. The growth rate is at its highest and there is enough flexibility to allow fluctuation over a relatively wide basin of attraction." The third phase is *saturation,* where "an increasing proportion of resources is devoted to maintenance and repair, and a declining proportion to structure-building."[i]

**Insurance leverage (a key concept).** Leverage is defined here as a ratio: the dollar amount of total health care spending divided by the out-of-pocket spending for all health care services (intuitively the average consumer's bang per buck). Coverage is the complement of leverage; in other words, the insurance portion of health care spending. In general, leverage=1/ portion of total spending out-of-pocket or 1/(1—coverage). If, on average, health care is covered half by consumer payments and half by insurance, leverage =1/0.5=1/(1-0.5)=2. In 1948, on average, insurance leveraged $1 out-of-pocket to buy $1.41 worth of health care services, so that leverage was 1.41; by 1960, $1 leveraged $1.98 of health care spending. Subsequent coverage growth led to $1 leveraging $2.97 in 1972, $4.25 in 1984, $6.34 in 1996, and $7.46 in 2009. One might think of the latter as a typical $20 copay leveraging an average of $149 in personal health care spending.[ii] Graph 4 shows historical average leverage levels for 1948-2009.

Dr. Edgar A. Peden

## Graph 4

## The Insurance Leverage of Out-of-Pocket Spending on Total Health Care Spending

Leverage (total spent on health care for $1 spent out-of-pocket)

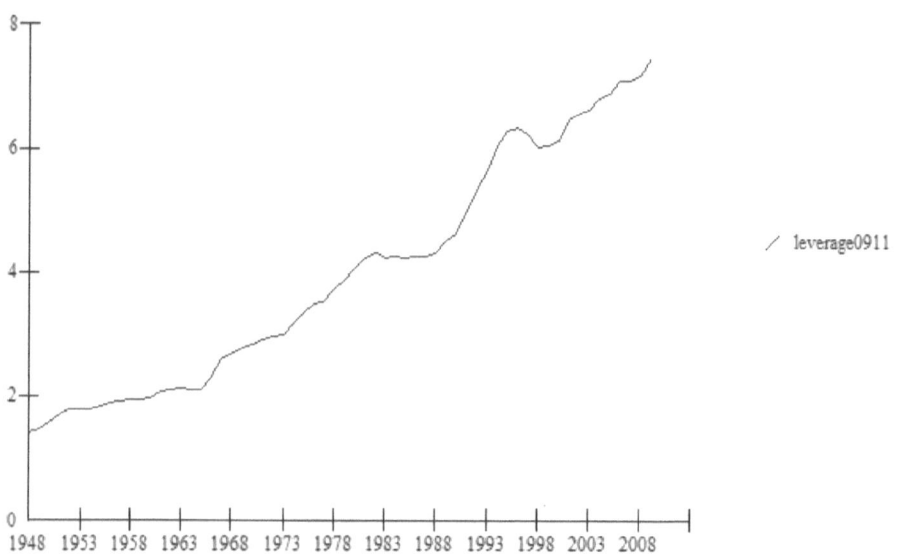

If there is truth in the old saying that 'he who pays the piper calls the tune', one would expect that, as leverage rises, patients would have less control over the type, quality and quantity of care received, and the insurers greater control as leverage rises.

**An S-curve equation.** F&W posit a logistic diffusion equation to capture the self-organization of the percentage of bank deposits accounted for by Australian Building Society deposits, that is:

Growth in $X_{t-1 \text{ to } t} = b_1 \cdot [1 - \{X_{t-1}/K(...)\}] + b(...) + c_1 \cdot$ Growth in $X_{t-2 \text{ to } t-1}$,
(1)

where $X$=Building Society deposits/M4, $b_1$=the underlying net diffusion rate, and b( . . .) and K( . . .) are functions of exogenous variables. In this formulation, F&W assume that the capacity limit (the top of the S-curve in graph 3, i.e. 'the saturation' of $X$) will be a function of K*( . . .), where the latter is determined by exogenous variables.

Foster tells us separately that "[t]ypically the b( . . .) function will contain factors that are 'short-period' in influence and the K( . . .) function will contain long-period' factors that determine the capacity limit to which structuration [in a self-organization process] will tend."[iii] Thus b( . . .) is a function specifying how other variables affect the growth in $X$.[20] This does not imply that the short-run b( . . .) term does not include variables with lagged effects, as the study shows below. Long-run structuration will usually be reflected in the K( . . .) term, although, as shown below, other factors, like managed care, reflect permanent changes in the health care market as well.

**Relative health care spending growth over the long-run.** This study posits that the F&W self-organizational S-curve, equation (1), comports closely with the trajectory of relative health care spending. The key assumption made is that K( . . .) is a function of insurance leverage.

The following historical information is germane to relative health care spending growth:

>1929-1946: Growth in relative health care spending was, for practical purposes, zero.

>1945: The 1942 rule change allowing employer-paid health insurance to be tax deductible during World War II was made permanent, creating an expansion of demand for both health care services and insurance,

---

[20] Both $b_1$ and $c_1$ are also parameters that may be a function of other variables, although in the estimated models found below they are not.

and creating incentives (1) for employers to procure insurance for their employees and (2) to increase the demand for health care providers selling their services.[21]

1948-1955: Relative health care spending began following an S-curve with its growth averaging 1.7 percent per year.

1955-1965: Growth in relative health care spending accelerated to average 2.7 percent per year.

However, seemingly counter to the F&W S-curve scenario, growth subsequently accelerated even more.

1965-1991: Growth averaged 3.0 percent per year.

What happened to the deceleration and saturation phase? This is where specification of the K( . . .) function becomes necessary.

**Hypothesis:** After the post-war punctuated change—that is, making the tax exclusion for employee health insurance permanent—the self-organization S-curve time path of relative health care spending itself became a direct function of insurance leverage, whereby over time increased leverage bent the relative health care spending trajectory upward to a new higher trajectory with greater growth all along the new trajectory. In terms of equation (1), K=K (leverage) and the whole S-curve grows faster when leverage increases.

Graph 5 shows a *hypothetical* S-curve for an assumed 1948 leverage level, and a faster-growing trajectory when leverage increased in 1970.

---

[21] No data were available for years prior to 1948.

## Graph 5

### Relative health care spending with hypothetical a leverage increase in 1970

**Health care spending as a percentage of consumption***

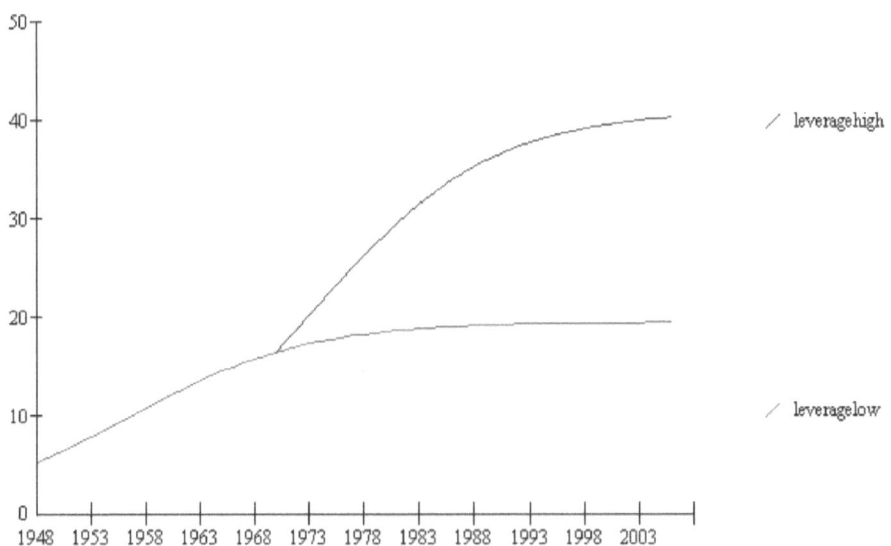

* The lower line indicates no change in leverage;

* The upper line shows an increase in leverage in 1970.

The lower trajectory in Graph 5 assumes that leverage is relatively low in 1948 with an average payment of under $1.50 for every dollar spent out-of-pocket. Assuming this stays the same, in the long-run, relative health care spending peaks out under 20 percent in the early 2000s. If the average payment jumps to $3.00 per dollar out-of-pocket in 1970, the S-curve branches to the upper trajectory of Graph 5 with higher growth thereafter, peaking at just above 40 percent.

The problem with Graph 5 is that it is hypothetical, although it goes a long way towards demonstrating how increases in leverage help explain how the average growth rates noted above (for 1948-1991), came about. Big changes in relative health care growth during the last two decades of this study's data were on the way, and these must be accounted for starting with the 1990s.

1991-2000: Growth averaged 0.2 percent per year.

This was the period during which managed care and government regulations became integral parts of the health care market, modifying its structure.

2001-2009: Growth averaged 2.3 percent per year.

During this last period, the previous decade's controls appeared to be offset by further increases in leverage levels and additional government programs. Blending all the relevant changes together over the full period requires an evolutionary modeling and statistical analysis is necessary to estimate the cause-and-effect relationships present in the 1948-2009 data.

**Evolutionary modeling and statistical analysis.** The F&W model applied to relative health care spending posits self-organization expressions (S-curves), like those in Graphs 3 and 5, which are continuous functions reflecting an "*endogenous theory of historical process.*"[liii] It is self-organized growth for the historical period and subject to econometric estimation.[liv] However, it is necessary to introduce other germane factors to allow these econometric estimates to approximate the trajectory of relative health care spending.

## Independent variables used in equation (1)

*Leverage effects take time.* Innovations within the health care sector come out of a never-ending stream of new ideas that provide investment options. R&D turns those ideas-into new and sometimes higher-quality products and services. Higher expected payoffs—inherent in greater leverage—make investment more likely, while the actual payoffs occur only after a long delay.[22]

### The K( . . .) term.

i. Leverage.

Relative health care spending growth is expected to vary directly with the lagged leverage level, so that K(leverage$_{t-z}$), where t is the current period and z is the number of years lagged in the self-organization diffusion function part of equation (1).

### The [b( . . .)] terms.

*Variables affecting growth on a more or less permanent basis.*

ii. Market power: managed care, insurance plans, and government.

After it became a factor in the early 1990s, managed care and other associated changes appear to have acted on a year-to-year basis to lower growth permanently (possibly with varying impacts as managed care rules, insurance rules, and government regulations keep changing).

---

[22] Sometimes new innovations, which are often designed to capture the additional insurance dollars available, face burdensome and costly bureaucracy, regulations, and administrative procedures.

*iii. Age-gender.*

Relative health care spending will vary directly with a government age-gender cost index. Thus relative health care spending *growth* will vary directly with this index's *growth*.[lv]

*iv. Non-commercial research spending.*

Government research augments medical R&D to develop innovative new services. Relative health care spending *growth* is posited to vary directly with *lagged growth* in the ratio of exogenous nominal non-private health care research spending to nominal net domestic product;[lvi] that is, the portion of total production (gross domestic product net of depreciation) devoted to medical R&D. We would expect that higher growth of this ratio would result in greater relative health care spending growth.

*Variables affecting growth in the short-run.*

*v. Adjusted coinsurance rate growth.*

Relative health care spending growth is posited to vary inversely with the growth in the adjusted coinsurance rate (the portion of health care spending consumers pay out-of-pocket after accounting for the tax break). This term is comparable to the one capturing the insurance effects in the Rand health insurance study, hereafter "the Rand experiment."[lvii] To date, the results of this study are the most cited benchmarks against which the results of other studies are compared.[23]

---

[23] Quoting Santerre, RE and Neun SP, Health Economics: Theories, Insights, and Industry Studies, Irwin, Chicago, 1996, "The RAND Health Insurance Study (HIS) is without a doubt the most comprehensive study . . . . . . [of] the impact of insurance on the demand for health care . . . to date. Families from six sites [around the US] were enrolled in various types of health insurance plans in a controlled experiment to test the impact of differences in insurance coverage on the demand for medical care."

*vi. Income.*

Both health care spending and other consumption growth vary strongly and directly with real per capita income growth.[24][lviii] But one would expect the income effect on health care spending to be proportionately much less than that on most other consumption, since health care is an economic necessity, like food and shelter. This implies a negative—but less than proportional—income *growth* effect (elasticity) on relative health care spending *growth*, because people will use increased income to buy fewer necessities relative to other consumption. Some studies, using mainly aggregated cross-country data, find a strong positive elasticity of income growth on relative health care spending growth.[lix] However, they do not control for health care insurance and its leverage—as is done here—or for government control of their country's health care systems.

*vii. Unemployment.*

Both health care spending and other consumption growth will vary inversely with unemployment, with the former—again because it is a necessity—affected proportionately less than the latter. Thus, relative health care spending *growth* is posited to vary inversely with the *unemployment rate*, but with an elasticity of less than one.[25]

---

[24] For my regression work, I use permanent real per capita income calculated following Milton Friedman's A Theory of the Consumption function, Princeton University Press, 1957, and as applied by Holt's two parameter estimation found in Pindyck, RS and DL Rubinfeld, Econometric Models and Economic Forecasts, Mc Graw-Hill Book Co., 1991, p 429.

[25] As this book is being written, the US economy., is experiencing a severe recession. Many are losing their jobs and their health insurance or are having to take jobs that have no insurance. This may be mitigated by the new Affordable Health Care Act of 2010. The inverse unemployment effect on relative health care spending may be offset to some degree during a downturn because some insurance continues to be paid under COBRA (the Consolidated Omnibus Budget Reconciliation Act), and because a

*viii. Lagged dependent variable.*

In their paper, "Econometric modeling in the presence of evolutionary change," F&W view "the presence [of a lagged dependent variable] as evidence of momentum."[lx]

## The dependent variable

*Relative health care spending growth year by year (1955-2009)*[26]

The variable, relative health care spending by year is constructed as follows. PHC spending is taken from the NHE accounts and includes spending for acute care (hospitals, physician services, prescription drugs, and other professional services), post-acute care (nursing homes, home health, and durable medical equipment), and sundry other categories (dentists and other personal health care). To get relative health care spending for each year, PHC is divided by PCE from BEA.[lxi] In the actual econometric work, relative health care spending growth is adjusted for age-gender factors prior to running the regression.[27]

---

number of government health care programs are counter-cyclical (e.g. Medicaid).

[26] Potentially it would have been possible to use data for the post-war period, 1948-2009. However, since the independent variables have up to 7-year lags, 1948-49 through 1954-55 were omitted, so that the regressions below encompass 1955-56 through 2008-09.

[27] Age and gender differences affect the rate that health care is consumed. For instance, an aged population demands more health care services than others. The Centers for Medicare and Medicaid Services (CMS), Office of the Actuary, has developed age-gender intensity and utilization indexes that reflect changing quantity demanded based on age and gender, indexes that affect PHC and thus the PHC percentage of PCE. Conceptually these indexes might be thought of as ordinary independent variables in a test equation, however, their effects are well enough established so that they can be used to directly adjust PHC and thus the PHC percentage of PCE to get an adjusted PHC percentage of PCE. Similarly, growth in the adjusted $PHC_{t-1\,to\,t}$ percentage of $PCE_{t-1\,to\,t}$ becomes an independent variable. A second, very minor, adjustment is made to

A problem with using two sources (NHE and BEA) for the two parts of the data is that PHC data from the NHE and aggregate PCE from the BEA are not exactly commensurable, as they use sources that differ slightly from one another. A recent paper, "A reconciliation of health care expenditures in the National Health Expenditures accounts and in gross domestic product," discusses these differences, concluding, "The estimates of total national health spending in the [NHE] and in the GDP data are relatively similar; they differ by less than 2 percent in most years back to 1960 . . . . This similarity is not surprising as the two accounts measure spending for a similar set of medical goods and services and rely on many of the same data sources."[lxii] Perhaps the best way to think of relative health care spending may not be as a percentage, but as the opportunity cost of consumption in general.

---

the dependent variable when we add government health spending (e.g. VA spending), not included in BEA's consumption measure, into overall consumption.

# 4. Empirical results

## Table 2[28]
### Regression results for the full period
Using all independent variables to estimate the modified diffusion equation

$$(1955-1956, \ldots, 2008-2009)^{\mu}$$

Growth in the adjusted health care spending percentage of consumption$_{t-1 \text{ to } t}$[29] =

### Lagged Dependent Variable

0.0392 · Growth in the adjusted health care spending percentage of consumption$_{t-2 \text{ to } t-1}$
(0.102)

### Self-organizational Diffusion Variable

+0.114 · [1 − {Adjusted health care spending percentage of consumption$_{t-1}$/ 9.128 · leverage$_{t-6}$}]
(0.019)***                                                                                         (2.136)***

### Lagged Growth in Relative Health Care Research Spending

+0.052 · Growth in research spending percentage of net domestic product$_{t-7 \text{ to } t-6}$
(0.026)**

### Point of Purchase Variables

−0.184 · Growth in the adjusted coinsurance rate$_{t-2 \text{ to } t-1}$$^{\mu\mu}$
(0.059)***

−0.588 · Growth in real per capita permanent income$_{t-1 \text{ to } t}$ $^{\mu\mu\mu}$
(0.142)***

−0.0052 · The unemployment rate$_{t-1}$
(0.0013)***

### Insurance Managed Care (including Government) Variable

−0.0316 · Managed care dummy variable$_{t}$
(0.0053)***.

---

[28] The adjustment is discussed above.

Unadjusted $R^2$ = 0.715. Durbin-Watson statistic (DW)=1.87. For the lagged variables, the numbers of lags, were estimated along with the parameters to minimize the sum of square errors.

µ   Standard errors of parameters in parentheses.

µµ   The adjustment is discussed in the description of this independent variable.

µµµ  This variable was estimated, along with the other parameters as part of the regression; as shown in the appendix, the adjustment parameter used to arrive at permanent income is itself 0.58, and should not be confused with the −0.588 coefficient of (post-adjustment) real per capita permanent income growth. The second parameter used in the Holt method to calculate permanent income shown in the Appendix and was estimated to be 1.0.

\* Indicates statistical significance at the 10 percent level;
\*\* indicates statistical significance at the 5 percent level; and
\*\*\* indicates statistical significance at the 1 percent level.

Table 2 shows the results of the regression results for the full-period. This regression was run using weighted non-linear least squares, where the weights reflect two different time periods. I distinguish between the two time periods because of a 1980 revision of the NHE accounts that improved the reliability of the data from 1980 on.[29] However, when the regressions were run on the split sample (1955-1956 through 1979-1980 and 1980-1981 through 2008-2009), the residuals prior to 1980 were slightly smaller than those from 1980 and later. Thus, when the full-period regression was run, I weighted observations through 1980 slightly more than the observations after 1980 (ratio=1.00:0.87). Thus as shown in the appendix, the data were split into two parts and the regression was re-run for each: 25 observations for 1955-1956 through 1979-1980, and 29 observations for 1980-1981 through 2008-2009.

This procedure also allows one to see if the results of Table 2 are consistent across subgroups of data. The two regressions had $R^2$s of 0.71 and 0.73 respectively, and the corresponding coefficients were not significantly different from one another. However, three differences must be noted. First, the second regression contained the managed care dummy variable, since its effect was confined to the latter period. Second, growth in the ratio of noncommercial medical research spending to net domestic product was much more variable during the first period when its estimated effect was positive and marginally significant,—than during the second period—when its estimated effect was positive but near zero. Third, the effect of the lagged dependent variable was negative for the first-period regression and near zero in the second-period regression, as it was overall.

### Effects of the independent variables

i. *Self-organization (leverage) S-curve variable.*

---

[29] Personal communication with Katherine Levit, Office of the Actuary, CMS.

Table 2 shows that lagged leverage *levels* [leverage(-6)][30] have had a highly significant positive effect on relative health care spending *growth*; increasing levels caused the relative health care spending time path to rise, more than offsetting the natural tendency of growth (for a given leverage) to slow as the market matures.[31], [32] It's highly significant positive coefficient, 9.128, implies that, as its driver, leverage(-6), rose, the relative health care spending time path (S-curve) was bent repeatedly upward, and its growth repeatedly increased.[33], [lxiii] Graph 6 shows simulated relative health care spending time-paths for leverage(-6) in 1955 (the first data year of my analysis) with discrete jumps every 10 years to their values for 1965, 1975, and so on. [34]

---

[30] The term leverage(-6) refers to the leverage level six years prior to the observation year.

[31] A previous paper, Peden and Freeland, 1998, found a highly significant leverage/coverage effect on acute care spending, a portion of personal health care spending. In both papers a six-year lag was optimal.

[32] Testing for the distributed lag effects of leverage, I found the distributions to be unstable due to collinearity between lagged leverage levels, although the sum of lagged effects was nearly equal to the effect of leverage lagged six years.

[33] While a six-year lag maximized our explanatory power, other lags have almost the same explanatory power, as seen in the high correlations of leverage (−6) with alternatives (e.g., a correlation of 0.982 with an 11-year lag. This was also seen in Peden and Freeland, 1998, which found that a six-year lag gave the best fit. We experimented there with distributed lagged effects for coverage (i.e. leverage), but found the distributions on the lagged effects unstable, and their sums nearly identical to a single six-year lag. That paper analyzed acute care spending, a subset of the PHC spending used here.

[34] The self-organizing/ diffusion equation from which Graph 6 was derived is as follows:

Health care spending percentage of consumption$_t$ =

Health care spending percentage of consumption$_{t-1}$ · [1 + b · (1 − {Health spending percentage of consumption$_{t-1}$/ k · leverage$_{t-6}$})], where b = 0.114 and k = 9.13. This equation gives us the dynamic formulation of relative health spending using only changes in the self-organization/ diffusion variable of the equation.

## Graph 6

## Simulations for Discrete Leverage Level Increases *

## Health Care Spending Percentage of Consumption

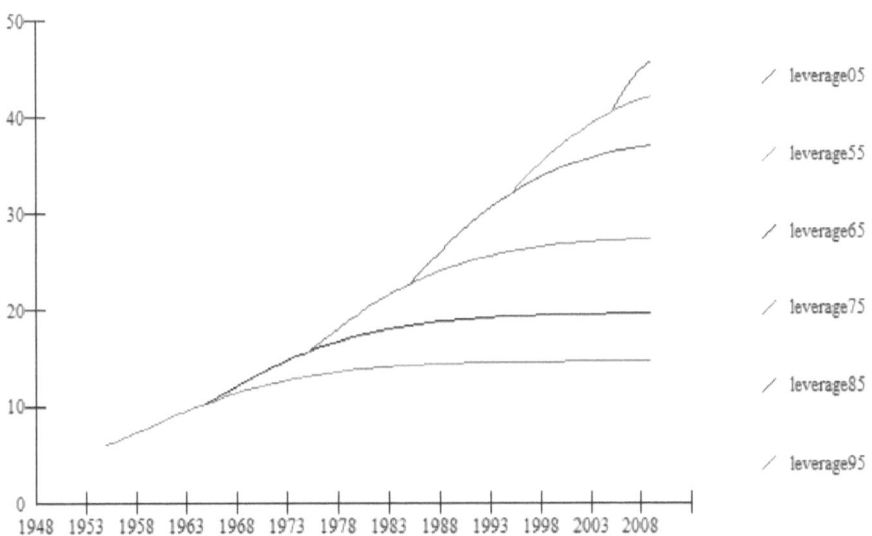

\* Leverage(-6) 1955: 1.46 (the lower line), 1965: 1.95, 1975: 2.78, 1985: 3.86, 1995: 4.52, to 2005: 6.03 (the highest line). The 10-year intervals are for illustration purposes; in fact changes occurred each year.

For leverage(-6) = 1.46 (the germane 1955 level) relative health care spending is simulated to rise from its 1955 level, 6.0 percent, ultimately reaching about 15 percent in 2009. For leverage(-6) = 1.95, the 1965 level (and second lowest path), relative health care spending rises ultimately to nearly 20 percent, and so on for higher leverage levels. The highest path shown [leverage(-6) = 6.03, the 2005 level] reaches 43 percent and is climbing. If not for offsetting factors (unemployment, income growth, and managed care, see below) rising leverage levels would have resulted in even higher relative health care spending.

Out-of-sample projection is, as always in statistical analysis, highly uncertain. However, relative health care spending was 20.9 percent in 2009, indicating that it is far below the S-curve saturation level estimated using just the leverage lagged six years, which in 2009 was 6.63. Even more important, is what it portends: by 2009 the leverage level had climbed to 7.46, implying that leverage should be a strong stimulus to relative health care spending growth for some time to come. It is undoubtedly because health care spending growth has continued at such a fast pace that health care reform—such as the enactment of the Affordable Care Act of 2010—continued to be such an important political issue in the U.S. after 2009.

ii. *Insurance, managed care, and government restrictions.* Managed care and government restrictions along with negotiations with providers to control spending growth resulted in a highly significant reduction in relative health care spending growth, starting in the early 1990s. The managed care dummy variable's cumulative coefficient, -3.3, implies that relative health care spending growth averaged 3.3 percentage points lower for each year from 1992-1993 through 2008-2009.[35] Before these restraints, in 1989-1990 and 1990-1991, growth in relative health care spending was 4.7 and 5.7 percent, respectively.[lxiv] Thus insurance, managed care, and government restrictions accounted for most of the essentially zero growth rate for 1991-2000.[36]

Some view these restrictions as first slowing relative health care spending growth, but losing their impact in the early 2000s. Positive residuals for 2000-2001 through 2002-2003 seem to support this view. However, residuals for 2003-04 through 2007-2008 are small and negative, only

---

[35] For 1991—92 the managed care dummy variable was 0.5 implying an effect of -1.6 percentage points for that transition year.
[36] Relative health care spending was a little above 17 percent for each of these years, averaging 17.3 percent overall.

turning positive for 2008-09. In any case, the regulatory environment seems now to be part of the accepted norm.[37] After 2000, other factors were also working, the most important of which were the continuing leverage increases. As shown below in the simulations of Table 3, it was the latter, along with lower unemployment, that caused relative health care spending growth to re-accelerate.[38]

*iii. Age-gender index.* Relative health care spending growth varied proportionately with the growth of this index, which averaged 0.3 percent per year from 1960 through 2009 (the years for which these data are available).[39]

*iv. Growth research spending as a proportion of net domestic product.*[lxv] Table 2 shows this ratio's growth had a positive effect—albeit lagged seven-years—on relative health care spending growth. This variable (defined as growth in the medical research spending portion

---

[37] The new health care reform bill passed in 2010 may represent yet another turning point upward—if and when it becomes fully enforced.

[38] Section 2, Table 1, showed that relative medical consumption (medical consumption/total consumption) grew over the years, both because of the rise in relative real medical spending and rises in relative medical prices where relative real medical spending=real medical consumption/ total real consumption. [Note: Real medical consumption=health care spending/ (the medical care PCE index), and total real consumption=total consumption/ (the overall PCE index)]. However, the managed care period brought a change in the relative importance of real consumption and price changes. Pre-managed care, 1955-1991, real relative medical consumption grew 0.6 percent per year and relative medical prices 2.3 percent. With managed care, 1992-2009, real relative medical consumption fell slightly (-0.04 percent per year), while relative medical prices grew 1.2 percent per year. Thus managed care and regulatory practices slowed relative health spending growth by reducing both real medical consumption growth: -0.6 percentage points per year to near 0 for this period, and relative medical price growth: 2.3 to 1.2 (or -0.9 percentage points per year). Again, we are dealing with fallible price indexes, but this has been true all through the 1948-2009 period examined and the magnitudes of the changes are overwhelming.

[39] Years prior to 1960 are predictions based on the trend at that time.

of net domestic product) had its greatest variation in the pre-1980 period. Up until that time, its average increase was nearly 7 percent per year, but after 1980 it averaged 1.8 percent per year. When the regression was run, either un-weighted for the full period or just through 1980, it was positive and marginally significant.

My conjecture is that, while it was an important factor in the early part of the data period, it has become less significant, compared with other factors driving relative health care spending growth. When queried, the late William Sobaski—a long time health care analyst during most of the data period examined—explained the importance of public spending for health care research (mainly by the National Institutes of Health) as a driver of relative health care spending growth during the period before the advent of Medicare and Medicaid in the mid to late 1960s. He described such spending, as essentially the "only thing" in the public sphere acting to stimulate this growth.[40] Since that time, the ratio's effect has diminished considerably in relative importance as a driver of health care spending growth.[41]

### Point-of-purchase variables

v. *Adjusted coinsurance growth.* Adjusting for the insurance tax break, coinsurance rate growth had a highly significant negative effect on relative health care spending growth, as expected from previous studies. Its coefficient from Table 2, -0.18, is in the range of the RAND experiment estimates, from -0.22 to -0.17.[lxvi] Using the average yearly growth of the adjusted coinsurance rate, -0.026, one finds its average effect

---

[40] Personal communication from Mr. Sobaski to the author, circa 1995.
[41] The long seven-year lag of this ratio on relative health spending is supported by the work of David Salkever and others. See Salkever, DS, "A Microeconomic Study of Hospital Cost Inflation," Journal of Political Economy, Vol. 80. No. 6 (November—December 1972) pp. 1144—1166. And again, it may reflect a distributed lag.

on relative health care spending growth was +0.5 percentage points per year (-0.18 · -0.026).

vi. *Income growth.* Real per capita permanent income growth has had a highly significant negative effect on relative health care spending growth. Its negative coefficient, −0.59,[42] implies that it disproportionately affects increases in short-run spending on goods and services other than health care, confirming that health care is *a necessity*, not a luxury. A typical 2.2 percent real income growth causes relative health care spending to grow −1.3 percentage points (-0.59 · 0.022). On the other hand, some consider health care a preferred good—one that people will buy more of as income rises. Both may be true! A strong positive effect of lagged real per capita permanent income was found for overall insurance coverage in regression (3a) in the appendix. Higher incomes thus imply smaller relative out-of-pocket health care spending vis-à-vis other consumption, but greater health care spending through insurance.

vii. *Unemployment.* This variable has a highly significant negative effect on relative health spending growth; its coefficient was -0.0052. This business cycle variable—countering the effects of real per capita income growth—implies that economic peaks (low unemployment) affect relative health care spending growth positively. If unemployment drops, say from 6 to 5 percent, relative health care spending growth rises 0.52 percentage points (-0.52 · [6-5]).

### *Simulated independent variable effects*

Above, I discussed each independent variable's effects separately. In Table 3, results from Table 2 are used to distribute relative health care spending growth effects by each of the

---

[42] After adjusting for the lagged dependent variable.

independent variables for 1955-2009 and 2000-2009. These simulations treat the age-gender adjuster as an independent variable (coefficient=1).

## Table 3

### Estimated Independent Variable: Average Effects on the Dependent Variable[43]

|  | 1955-2009 Yearly Average(%) | 2000-2009 Yearly Average(%) |
|---|---|---|
| **Dependent Variable:** | | |
| Growth in relative health care spending$_{t-1\ to\ t}$ | 2.3 | 2.3 |
| **Independent Variables:** | | |
| Age-gender changes$_{t-1\ to\ t}$ | 0.3 | 0.4 |
| Self-organization diffusion expression with leverage$_{t-6}$ | 6.9 | 8.0 |
| Growth in research percentage of net domestic product$_{t-8\ to\ t-7}$ | 0.2 | 0.1 |
| Growth in the coinsurance rate$_{from\ t-2\ to\ t-1}$ | 0.5 | 0.4 |
| Growth in real per capita permanent income$_{t-1\ to\ t}$ | -1.3 | -0.9 |
| Unemployment rate$_{t-1}$* | -3.1 | -2.8 |
| Managed care dummy variable$_t$ | -1.1 | -3.3 |
| Explained | 2.4 | 1.9 |
| Unexplained | -0.1 | 0.4 |

---

[43] The effects of the lagged dependent variable are subsumed in the effects of the individual independent variables.

**The full period.** Average yearly relative health care spending growth (1955-1956 through 2008-2009) was 2.3 percent. The dominant stimulus to this growth has been the self-organization diffusion (leverage) variable, averaging +6.9 percentage points per year as seen in Table 3. Other effects included growth in the ratio of medical research spending to net domestic product: +0.2 percentage points, the managed care dummy, -1.1 percentage points; real per capita permanent income growth, -1.3 percentage points, coinsurance growth, 0.5 percentage points; age-gender effects, 0.3 percentage points and unemployment, -3.1 percentage points.[44]

**2000-2009.** These simulations are shown in the right-hand column of Table 3. During this period, relative health care spending growth was +2.3 percent per year, the same as the full-period (1955-2009) average. The primary cause of relative health care spending growth was again the positive effect of the self-organization/diffusion variable driven by ever-higher leverage(-6) levels. However, whereas its stimulus averaged +6.9 percentage points per year for 1955-2009, during 2000-2009 it was +8.0 percentage points per year. The ratio of noncommercial research spending to net domestic product was but a small factor.[45] Age-gender factors induced an average growth of +0.4 percentage points, a small bump up from its historic impact, undoubtedly due to an aging population. Coinsurance growth had about the same impact as it did historically (+0.4 vs. +0.5 percentage points per year for the latter). Real per capita permanent income growth had a smaller negative effect in this latest period, -0.9 vs. -1.3 percentage points overall. Unemployment, averaged 5.8 percent historically

---

[44] Unemployment was high for the sub-period from the mid-1970s to the mid-1980s, undoubtedly slowing relative health spending growth and adding heavily to its overall induced average growth rate of −3.1 percentage points per year.

[45] As noted above, appendix equation (3a) estimates indicate that prior to 1980, growth in the research spending to net domestic product ratio may have accounted for relative health care spending growth for up to 0.5 percent per year; this would explain its diminishing relative importance over time.

vs. 5.0 percent from 2000 through 2009; its negative impact thus fell slightly from -3.1 for the full-period to -2.8 percentage points per year. Managed care and government restrictions had an effect of -3.3 percentage points per year effect on relative health care spending in the latest period vs. -1.1 for the whole period.[46]

**Perspective.** Relative health care spending growth for 2000-2009 reflects—to a large extent—the opposing effects of leverage increases and regulatory constraints. This is like driving a car while stepping on the gas (leverage) and brake (regulatory constraints) at the same time. Comparing the middle and right-most columns of Table 3 for each shows their increased (opposing) effects. This tension reflects complex opposing stakeholder interactions governing crucial health care sector decisions. Besides patients, providers, insurance plans, and local, state and federal governments, stakeholders include provider and academic associations, patients' public interest groups, labor unions, and research institutions, the latter including governments at all levels. Health care rent-seeking is alive and well in the U.S.[47]

In evolutionary terms, given the increases in volatility apparent in Graph 2 in the most recent five decades and the uncertainty of the level of government involvement in the health care sector, this sector may be headed toward a structural discontinuity that will subtly or strongly modify the trajectory of the post-WWII period. Given that the managed care and government regulatory changes of the early 1990s were very effective in slowing relative health care spending growth, after which the first decade of the 2000s saw a strong resumption of this growth, one might anticipate further moves

---

[46] After all, its full effect was not felt until the early 1990s.
[47] Rent seeking is the activity of anyone trying to achieve or maintain a monopoly in order to gain monopoly profits, or 'rent'. The rent-seeking paradigm is the brain-child of Professor James Buchanan and his disciples, Anne Krueger and Gordon Tullock. Often it involves stakeholders in the institutions listed above seeking to manipulate government rules and regulations on their own behalf.

toward centralized control of health care and its spending by government—something that would come to pass with the Affordable Care Act of 2010. Sorting this out will be the job of future econometric work.

## Two views supporting the role of insurance as a health care spending driver.

A recent paper by Amy Finkelstein,[lxvii] mainly using Medicare hospital data, suggests that "the overall spread of health insurance between 1950 and 1990 may be able to explain about half of the increase in real per capita health care spending over this period." Taking out the propensity of health care spending to grow along with other spending as income rises, I assume that Finkelstein's portion is even higher after the effects of income are removed. She concludes that " . . . Medicare is associated with a 37 percent increase in real hospital expenditures (for all ages) between 1965 and 1970. This estimate is over six times larger than what evidence from the impact of an individual's health insurance would have predicted." Here she is suggesting that the spread of health care insurance may have played a much larger role in the growth of health care spending than the "gold standard" Rand experiment would suggest. Her basic insight is that market-wide changes in health care insurance may have fundamentally different effects on the health care sector than what short-run neoclassical analyses (like the Rand experiment) would imply. The above results imply a strong agreement between what Finkelstein found and the findings of the current study.

This brings one back to the fundamental distinction between Marshall's short-run and long-run analyses and his warning against extending the former when the latter is needed. Finkelstein seems to take the longer view, as does the current study.[48]

---

[48] Other studies are supportive of a strong long-term relationship between insurance and health spending. Finkelstein mentions two: Martin Feldstein's "Hospital Cost Inflation: A Study of Nonprofit Dynamics",

A final study by Garber, Jones, and Romer—which focuses mainly on the drug industry, but whose findings can be generalized—concludes that:

The subsidy to demand inherent in the low copayment leads to excess profits in many cases. The resulting dynamic inefficiency raises the possibility that finite patent lives [of products and services] could be welfare improving by reducing excessive innovation.

Furthermore, if drug prices increase too quickly with the decline in coinsurance rate, insurers may not lower out-of-pocket costs enough to get benefiting patients to consume the drugs they need.[lxviii]

---

American Economic Review, LXI, (1971), 853-872. and "Quality Change and the Demand for Hospital Care," Econometrica, XLV (1977), 1681-1702. And Feldstein, M and A Taylor, The Rapid Rise of Hospital Costs," Staff Report of the Council of Wage and Price Stability, Executive Office of the President, 1977,. In addition, my colleague and I noted two other studies in our previous paper, Weisbrod, BA "The Health Care Quadrilemma: An Essay on Technological Change, Insurance, Quality of Care and Cost Containment." Journal Of Economic Literature 29(1991) 523-552. Also see Bradley, R "Growth of U.S. health care spending." Contemporary Economic Policy 12 (1994) 45-56. It is surprising that in the face of all the evidence to the contrary, some estimators continue to use the short-term Rand experiment results for their long-term estimates.

## 5. Conclusion

**The legacy of a rule change.** D&P tell us that economic evolution can be defined as the process by which the knowledge base of the economy changes. This happens as novel rules are originated, adopted and retained by carriers, thus changing their operational capabilities.[lxix] It is hard to imagine a rule change that has had effects as far reaching as the post-WWII decision to make the employer income tax exclusion for employee health care insurance permanent. The reactions to this rule change appear to have initiated the series of increases in insurance coverage, relative medical prices, and relative health care spending, as the health care sector has organized in an autocatalytic way to generate and then re-generate these increases for nearly seven decades. A host of new agents have entered this sector because of the increased financial incentives that resulted from the rise in relative spending for health care. Most prominently these agents include providers, the government and insurance companies (in their multiple forms), and special interests representing both consumers and providers of care. Regulation has also brought the legal profession into health care as disputes have arisen over what is covered and for how much. A large (and growing) bureaucracy has arisen to handle the checks, counterchecks, and clearances necessary to provide medical services.

**The historical experience (1948-2009).** To provide a background for concerns about continuing relative health care spending growth and the lack of access to care, this study has analyzed health care spending from 1948 through 2009, when it went from 5.3 to 20.9 percent of consumption. Its central statistical finding is that this rise was generated by continuing increases in insurance coverage, first allowed by the single rule change in after 1945. In evolutionary terms, this initial rule change—a continuation of the WWII employer tax exclusion for employee health care insurance—resulted in a punctuated equilibrium. The subsequent autocatalytic reactions included ever-expanding levels of coverage which, in turn, led to relative growth in both health care spending and medical prices. This then fed back to increase demand for more insurance, and then to increases in relative spending, higher prices, and so on. In the mid-1960s, government programs were initiated to cover the uninsured, starting with Medicare (for the aged) and Medicaid (for the poor); these programs were undoubtedly initiated to compensate for the increased spending by two of the primary groups of individuals left uncovered by insurance. The disabled were covered a few years later.

Even though managed care had been available during the 1980s, it became most effective during the early 1990s, as managed care and government market controls acted to partially offset the cost-increasing dynamic. However, after a nearly decade long hiatus, from 1993 to 2000, most of the decades long growth in relative health care spending continued anew, as seen on the front cover of the book. In addition, the market restrictions imposed before, during, and since the hiatus have continuingly intensified the burdens of both insurance company requirements and government regulations on health care market participants (both patients and providers), burdens not seen previously in the U.S. The resources used for rent-seeking and bureaucracy have led us away from a health care market whose primary purpose is to efficiently deliver services to patients needing care. Paraphrasing John Goodman,[lxx]

> With respect to the organization and financing of care, innovation is rampant. And wherever health insurers are paying the bills (almost 90% of the market) innovation has been of two forms: (1) initiating ways for providers to maximize their income given third-party reimbursement formulas or (2) initiating ways for third-party payers to minimize what they pay out. It is unclear what effects these innovations have on the quality of patient care received or its efficient delivery.

With the additional coverage passed recently under the Affordable Care Act of 2010, the U.S. is likely to see accelerating relative health care spending, like that shown in hypothetical

Graph 5 starting in 1970, including additional rent-seeking, bureaucracy, and administrative expenses. And these would be in addition to existing government regulations, including rationing and price controls.

Missing this historic picture is to miss not only the causes of the unwanted growth in relative health care spending, but also its dilatory effects,—in other words—the foregone consumption of other goods and services that also make life worthwhile.[49]

**The Impact of the Affordable Care Act.** So what might we have to look forward to from the Affordable Care Act of 2010 and its reaffirmation by the Supreme Court in 2012? For one thing, it is probable that the amount of health insurance coverage will increase dramatically. Part of this will assuredly be due to increased government spending, which Congressional Budget Office estimates indicate will increase federal spending by $1.1 trillion over the next decade.[lxxi] It may be a game changer the way Medicare and Medicaid were in the mid to late 1960s. Moreover, mandating insurance coverage must surely increase coverage. A mitigating factor would occur to the extent that individuals and firms elected to increase coverage using health savings accounts (HSAs) along with catastrophic coverage policies. On a positive note, one might expect that the needed "public good" safety net may improve.

**Policy Conclusions.** The primary purpose of this study has been to examine what has caused relative health care spending to rise as much as it has, using an evolutionary model estimated econometrically. The historical diffusion function I estimate suggests that insurance coverage and its growth are the primary cause of the inordinate growth of health spending

---

[49] In addition to the cost-raising effects of the Affordable Care Act of 2010, it may even curb access to health care itself, as mandated services (free annual checkups, free preventive services, and so on) crowd out access to primary care physicians. To understand how this may play out, see "Why the Doctor Can't See You," an editorial by John Goodman in the *Wall Street Journal*, August 15, 2012.

as part of consumption over the past six decades. However, the diffusion function is irreversible, and over this period what evolved is path dependent; the same is expected to be true in the future. The effects of the past 60-plus years cannot be undone. As a society, we will evolve from where we are. The question is, what policies should be adopted to ameliorate the current tendency to devote ever more of our national income to health care to the detriment of other desired consumption?

The historical analysis here and lessons learned from the work of other economists lead to several suggestions regarding policy changes. One clear lesson is that—as a society—we should not expand coverage, however well-intentioned, without being aware of what such expansion has done to relative health care spending, and especially relative medical prices, in the past.

I believe—as do other economists—that it is possible to develop policy recommendations that, if implemented, (1) would modify the health care and insurance sectors so they provide the services people value, but (2) would not reallocate an increasingly larger portion of consumption away from other goods and services that people also value. In other words, policy prescriptions should make the market for health care and insurance sectors function more efficiently and serve the needs that people have for their services more effectively.

More specifically, I propose a three-pronged approach: (1) introduce market discipline into the market for health care, (2) address the *public good* need for care for those who require care but are unable to procure it for themselves, and (3) expand the tax exclusion to include individuals and not just firms. A market discipline of sorts occurred in the 1990s under managed care, when people contracted with health care organizations to handle all of their health care needs. Because these organizations gained complete (or near complete) control over these individuals' health care consumption, they were able to economize in various ways; and, as shown above, the growth of relative health care spending was nearly zero for almost a decade before becoming positive once more.

But managed care also restricted the individual to his or her managed care plan and its rules.

For many, it was (and still is) "just what the doctor ordered," and it's not something that should be taken away from those who choose to enroll in it. On the other hand, there may be less intrusive ways to introduce market efficiency and discipline. Richard Nelson tells us that,[lxxii]

> . . . while a market as it actually is does not achieve "Pareto optimality," most economists and many lay persons would argue that market organization and competition often do seem to generate results that are moderately efficient. There are strong incentives for firms to produce goods and services that customers want, or can be persuaded they want, and to produce at as low a financial cost as is possible. Also, under many circumstances competitive market-organized economic sectors seem to respond relatively quickly to changes in customer demands, supply conditions, and technological opportunities. Thus, to the extent that producing what customers value is treated as a plus, and so long as factor prices roughly measure opportunity costs, there is a strong pragmatic case for market organization, broadly defined, on economic efficiency grounds . . .

**(1)** To this end, I suggest that policy makers consider HSAs (plus high deductible insurance policies) as one of the central mechanisms for future policy. When people spend their own money on health care services—and from whatever provider they choose—they value what they spend on a given service at least as much as they value the same amount of money spent elsewhere. Such a system should lead to marked efficiency improvements over the current system, where every $1 of their own that they spend leverages over $7.50 worth of services, on average. The money people spend out of an HSA for medical services is their own money un-supplemented by insurance payments. The benefits they receive are that their insurance premiums are much lower and they have the additional freedom of purchasing the health care they desire.

*Health Savings Accounts.* HSAs are individual accounts, where premiums paid by individuals and/or their employers are split into two parts: (1) a monthly amount to pay for a catastrophic plan and (2) a contribution to an individual HSA account. Premiums are tax deductible; contributions by employers (and others) are treated the same as premiums for traditional insurance policies and premiums paid by the self-employed. HSAs can be used to pay most discretionary medical expenses.[50] Monies in individual HSAs are owned by the individual and can accumulate indefinitely so they can be used for future medical expenses.[51] The high-deductible insurance part added to an HSA covers catastrophic medical expenses (above the deductible). First-dollar coverage for certain preventive and non-discretionary medical expenses might also be added; for example, an emergency appendectomy.[52] In sum, HSAs would accumulate savings like Individual Retirement Accounts, but out of which spending on health care would not be taxed.

Most traditional health care insurance policies require a copay for medical services. Insurance policies paying first-dollar coverage for services eliminate copays entirely (e.g. some managed care plans), while—on the other end of the spectrum—some catastrophic plans require that patients pay a large out-of-pocket payment for all medical services during a given year (e.g. $5000), but then the catastrophic plan pays everything above this given amount. As would be expected, premiums for the first are much higher than for the second.

---

[50] For example, physician visits, diagnostic tests, most prescription drugs, etc.
[51] Withdrawals from HSAs are taxable as income when used for non-medical purposes. If the individual dies, these monies are inheritable.
[52] John Goodman, president of The National Center for Policy Analysis publishes the daily blog HEALTH ALERT. He is the author or coauthor of numerous books on health economics and has been dubbed "The Father of HSAs."

It seems to me that something in between would be desirable for most people, at their discretion.

Would it not make sense for employers to allot a certain benefit amount to each employee, but then let them choose from a cafeteria of plans, such as those now available for federal employees? The options should include one consisting of a combination of an HSA, traditional insurance, and catastrophic insurance. Such a plan could allow an employee to put part of their health care insurance allotment money in an HSA so that, as her HSA savings grew and she could afford to pay more out-of-pocket for her own care, and she could gradually move towards whatever insurance combination she desired: traditional, HSA, and/or catastrophic coverage. She could even lower the non-employer portion of the premiums she has to pay herself.

I do not present a complete description of how HSAs would work and how they would apply to populations procuring medical care using them. For a fuller description, see Goodman, Goodman, Musgrave, and Herrick, and Goodman and Musgrave.[53], [lxxiii, lxxiv] HSAs should be attractive to a large number of working-age, particularly younger adults trying to build a nest egg to purchase medical care as they grow older, while at the same time providing insurance coverage for themselves and their families. A side-benefit of the buildup of HSA savings would be the alleviation of insurance-driven pressures on the demand for medical care.

HSAs should be available for all—employed, self-employed, and unemployed—on the same tax-exclusionary basis as employer-employee insurance is currently. Including HSAs as part of an overall plan ensures that full personal medical insurance is available for all, and as described by Pilzer, at

---

[53] Much work has already been done with respect to medical savings accounts (MSAs),—the precursor of HSAs—by these researchers. The difference between MSAs and HSAs is that the former have more restrictions on them.

much lower expense than traditional comprehensive coverage.[lxxv] When HSAs are optional for both employers and individuals, they will be chosen only if they are desired. One might object that employers could change the coverage they offer by adopting less costly HSAs (plus catastrophic insurance) and dropping more comprehensive coverage. However, it is generally known by labor economists that employers consider the entire cost of an employee—salary plus benefits plus other employment costs—in hiring and continuing employment decisions. If these costs rise, say, because of higher benefits, employers will, over time, pass these costs to employees in the form of lower wages. On the other hand, for any given dollar amount employers are willing to pay employees, lowering benefit costs—say by procuring a lower cost insurance plan like a rudimentary HSA plus catastrophic plan—will, over time, raise employee salaries.[lxxvi]

One might envision that employers, employees and individuals would have a tax incentive to create individual safety nets through contributions to HSAs. The savings in these accounts would build up over time just as the equity in a home does. Both HSAs and home equity may be considered part of a safety net for necessities required most of our lives. [54]

**(2)** *Public Good Aspects of Health Care.* Health care and health care insurance, as we have treated it thus far, for most people

---

[54] One way in which HSAs may result in a non-Pareto optimal outcome is where there are deliberate inequities in the premium structure accorded favored employees. For instance, if a firm employs a workforce with a variety of medical risks (say low-risk younger workers and high-risk older workers), where it currently pays an equal premium for each when the premium is based on the average risk across all workers. But the employees most likely not to choose HSA policies would be the high-risk employees who receive an implicit subsidy from the low-risk employees on all types of health insurance, including catastrophic coverage. Perhaps risk adjusting premiums for the non-HSA part of the insurance premium would be necessary to attract low-risk employees to opt for HSA accounts, albeit raising the relative premium cost per worker for currently higher-risk subsidized employees.

fits well within an evolutionary market approach applied to analyses of this sector. However, even though the market is generally the best allocator of resources, some functions cannot be done efficaciously by numerous participants in the market, and are best left to a central authority; orphans and those with severe disabilities come immediately to mind. Richard Nelson argues that:[lxxvii]

> [M]any goods and services are partly private and partly public, in the sense that there is an identifiable benefit to particular individuals, . . . [but] at the same time [a] broad atmospheric benefit from the [general] availability or provision of the good or service. Education is a prominent example. Vaccination for contagious diseases is another.

In modern society, many goods and services fit in this category. Food Stamps and charitable organizations providing basic food for needy families fit in this category, as does the provision of basic housing. The K–12 public schooling that children receive comes free of charge and has been highly successful in most instances. The need for some basic health care was instituted in the 1960s (Medicare and Medicaid), for the disabled in the early 1970s (under Medicare) and for children's health care in the early 2000s.[55] Again, as Nelson tells us, "'publicness'" resides in values defined in terms of perceptions about what makes a society a decent and just one."[lxxviii]

Just what a safety-net medical program should look like is the subject of on-going debate. The U.S. government's Medicaid and children's health care programs appear to be doing an adequate job in most instances. But a single-payer approach to health care has drawbacks, in that (1) it doesn't necessarily provide the care that many people (and their families and providers) find desirable, and (2) it allows people to shirk

---

[55] Numerous communities and states have put in place hospitals and other welfare facilities providing health care for over a century.

responsibilities to cover the medical costs they and their families incur, but may not need.

*Health Care R&D as a public good.* R&D is certainly central to health care innovation, and even here the market appears to be the best allocator of resources in most instances—although there are public good exceptions the market cannot handle efficaciously, such as research on rare diseases. On the whole, however, as Richard Nelson tells us,[lxxix]

> Centrally planned systems often have achieved strong success in allocating R&D resources where the objectives were sharply defined and the likely best routes to success quite clear. The Manhattan Project and Project Apollo are good examples. However, for the most part potential innovators are faced with the problem of guessing just how much users will value various innovations they might introduce, and also of judging how easy or difficult it would be to develop various alternatives. The answers to these questions seldom are clear. Further, well-informed experts are likely to disagree on the answers. Under these conditions, the competitive pluralism of market-organized R&D systems is a great advantage . . . . [T]he pluralism, flexibility, and competition of modern capitalism are surely essential aspects of any effective innovation system.

There is probably no better example of public good R&D in the health sector than The National Institutes of Health (NIH) and its sister agencies. Together with U.S. health care firms like the big pharmacy companies, and in cooperation with organizations in other countries (public and private), NIH stands at the center of medical knowledge in the U.S., both a repository of this knowledge and a sponsor of the medical research that benefits us all, and indeed those in other parts of the world as well.

**(3)** *A Final Policy Consideration: Expanding the Tax Exclusion to Individuals.* Allowing individuals to purchase health insurance on the same tax-deductible basis as employers would level the playing field between those employed by employers getting a tax break for the amount they spend for employees' health insurance and those who work for employers who don't provide such coverage. The latter commonly accomplish this by hiring people part-time or on a contract basis. Indeed John Goodman tells us in his tax blog of July 9, 2012, that this is a matter of tax fairness, as "people who must purchase their own insurance get little if any help from the IRS," and that those who earn less get a much smaller tax subsidy than high earners who tend to have greater, more inclusive and expensive, coverage. In addition, with the tax exclusion expanded to individuals, individual coverage would be portable, allowing people to move from job to job and in and out of the labor market.[56] Such control would enable consumers to choose between individual and group (including employer) policies and thus be full participants in the market for health insurance and, through their choices, be participants in the market for health care itself.

A more complete discussion of policy considerations than what follows from my evolutionary-econometric empirically based study is found in John C. Goodman's recent book, *Priceless: curing our health care crisis*,[lxxx] a valuable addition to his previous work.

**In summary.** This study has shown that greater insurance coverage results in increased in relative health care spending growth, which in turn results in even greater insurance coverage and then further increases in relative health care spending growth, and so on, in an autocatalytic pattern. With the phasing in of the provisions of the Affordable Care Act, which

---

[56] Goodman actually recommends replacing "the current system of tax and spending subsidies with a lump sum, refundable tax credit of $2,500 for every adult and $8,000 for a family of four. These credits would fund the core insurance that we want everyone to have. Additional coverage could be purchased by individuals and their employers with (unsubscribed) after-tax dollars."

expands coverage even more, the U.S. may be on the verge of accentuating this pattern further, sacrificing, yet again, more of the other types of consumption people value (e.g. housing, transportation, and food) as well as public goods which are also valued (e.g. military preparedness, education, roads, and law enforcement). Health care may soon begin crowding out these other goods and services, forcing individuals, firms, and government agencies to make some difficult decisions. As much as we'd all like to, we can't have everything.

# Appendix
## Table A-1

## Nonlinear least-squares estimate of equation (3) for two sub-periods

### Sub-period 1

*1955-1956 through 1979-1980 (standard errors in parentheses)*

(1a) Growth in the adjusted health care spending percentage of consumption$_{t-1\text{ to }t}$ =

**Lagged Dependent variable**
-0.277 · Growth in the adjusted health care spending percentage of consumption$_{t-2\text{ to }t-1}$
(0.14)**

**Self-organizational diffusion variable**
+0.103 · [1 - {adjusted health care spending percentage of consumption$_{t-1}$/26.693 · leverage$_{t-6}$}]
(0.044)**                                                                                     (58.30)

**Lagged growth in relative health care research spending**
+ 0.053 · Growth in research spending percentage of net domestic product$_{t-7\text{ to }t-6}$
(0.032)**

**Point of purchase variables**

- 0.138 · Growth in the adjusted coinsurance rate$_{t-2\text{ to }t-1}$
(0.081)**

- 0.672 · Growth in real per capita permanent income$_{t-1\text{ to }t}$
(0.188)***

- 0.00806 · The unemployment rate$_{t-1}$
(0.0021) ***

**Insurance/ managed care and government variable**
Not Applicable

Years 1955-1956 through 1979-1980. $R^2 = 0.714$. DW = 2.34. For this and the subsequent regression:

\* indicates statistical significance at the 10 percent level;
\*\* indicates statistical significance at the 5 percent level; and
\*\*\* indicates statistical significance at the 1 percent level.

## Table A-2

## Sub-period 2

1980-1981 through 2008-2009 (standard errors in parentheses):

(2a) Growth in the adjusted health care spending percentage of consumption$_{t-1 \text{ to } t}$ =

**Lagged Dependent variable**
0.031 · Growth in the adjusted health care spending percentage of consumption$_{t-2 \text{ to } t-1}$
(0.205)

**Self-organizational diffusion variable**
+0.141 · [1 - {adjusted health care spending percentage of consumption$_{t-1}$/5.78 · leverage$_{t-6}$}]
(0.028)***    (1.45)***

**Lagged growth in relative health research spending**
+ 0.010 · Growth in research spending percentage of net domestic product$_{t-7 \text{ to } t-6}$
(0.060)

**Point of purchase variables:**

- 0.258 · Growth in the adjusted coinsurance rate$_{t-2 \text{ to } t-1}$
(0.139)**

- 0.712 · Growth in real per capita permanent income$_{t-1 \text{ to } t}$
(0.336)**

- 0.00219 · The unemployment rate$_{t-1}$
(0.00265)

**Insurance/ managed care and government variable**
- 0.035 · Managed care dummy variable$_t$
(0.00769)***.

Years 1980-1981 through 2008-2009. $R^2 = 0.73$. DW = 1.87.

The two sub-period regressions (shown in Tables A-1 and A-2) are consistent in the signs and magnitudes of the coefficients of the separate variables, and although the coefficients of the coinsurance growth rate and the unemployment rate differ a bit, the difference is not statistically significant.[57] In general, these regressions support the results found in the full-period regression, Table 2.

**Coverage as a function of income and relative medical prices.** The coinsurance rate (the portion paid out-of-pocket) is posited to be determined by a number of factors: real per capita permanent income, the relative prices of medical care, and the percentage public within health care spending. One would expect all three to have a negative –coverage-increasing—effect on the coinsurance rate. This relationship is run using first differences, following a distributed lag specification containing a lagged dependent variable. Table 3 shows the results.

---

[57] I note here that the unemployment varied more during the first than the second period. The second period encompasses an additional insurance related variable, the managed care variable, which may have affected the impact of the growth in the adjusted coinsurance rate.

## Table A-3

### Nonlinear least-squares estimate of the growth of the coinsurance rate as a function of four causal growth rates

(3a) Gr in the adjusted coinsurance rate$_{t-1 \text{ to } t}$ =

0.323·gr in the adjusted coinsurance rate$_{t-2 \text{ to } t-1}$
(0.086)***

- 0.227·gr in relative medical prices$_{t-4 \text{ to } t-3}$
(0.139)*

- 0.343· gr in percentage health spending public$_{t-1 \text{ to } t}$
(0.046)***

- 0.322 · gr in permanent income$_{t-6 \text{ to } t-5}$
(0.131)***

1955-1956 through 2008-2009. $R^2$= 0.80, DW=1.82. The lag structure is chosen along with the coefficients of the independent variables.

This regression can be seen as a partial adjustment model of the Marshallian short-run.

Note that, because of the role played by real permanent income in determining the adjusted coinsurance rate, its effect will be understated in the regressions treating the lagged adjusted coinsurance rate as a (predetermined) independent variable. The latter's significance in equation (3a) implies that the growth in real permanent income has a negative impact on growth in the adjusted coinsurance rate, thus increasing coverage growth, albeit with a distributed lag between income growth and coinsurance growth. The elasticity of permanent income growth on the coinsurance growth rate over time is an estimated -0.476 (i.e., the combined income growth coefficient adjusted for the time lag, -0.322 · 1/[1 - 0.323], where 0.323 is the coefficient of the lagged dependent variable).

I also find that relative medical price growth played a similar role in determining coverage growth. The distributed lag elasticity of the growth of relative medical prices on growth in the adjusted coinsurance rate is an estimated -0.335 (i.e., the coefficient = -0.227 · 1/ [1 - 0.323]).

Finally, the growth in the percentage of health care spending that is public has a highly significant effect on coverage growth. Its effect over-time on the adjusted coinsurance rate growth is -0.507 (i.e. the coefficient = -0.343 · 1/ [1 - 0.323]).

**Estimating permanent real per capita disposable income.** Based on Friedman, I estimated permanent income using current and past actual income and two parameters: (1) for the speed at which permanent income adapts to actual income and (2) for the speed at which expected income growth adapts to permanent income growth. Equations (4a) and (5a) reflect Holt's two-parameter exponential smoothing method for this estimation:

$$\ln(G_{pt}) = \Gamma \cdot \ln(G_t) + (1 - \Gamma) \cdot [\ln(G_{pt-1}) + gr_e G_{pt-1}] \quad (4a)$$

$$gr_e G_{pt} = \varsigma \cdot [\ln(G_{pt}) - \ln(G_{pt-1})] + (1-\varsigma) \cdot gr_e G_{pt-1}, \quad (5a)$$

where $gr_e G_{pt}$ is expected growth in $G_{p\,t-1\,tot}$. The latter is estimated as $\ln(G_{pt}) - \ln(G_{pt-1})$ in equation (5a). Using 1931-2009 data $\Gamma$ and $\varsigma$ are chosen (range 0-1)—along with the other regression parameters—to minimize the sum of squared errors.

# Biographies

Edgar A. Peden is a retired U.S. government economist where he worked in the Veteran's Administration, the Congressional Budget Office, and the Centers for Medicare and Medicaid Services. He has a Bachelor of Arts degree in mathematics and a Master of Arts in economics from the University of Colorado. He went on to earn a second Masters and a Ph.D., both in economics, from The George Washington University, with a concentration in econometrics. He has published a number of empirical articles in macroeconomics and in health economics. During his time in the government, he became interested in and then studied the theory of evolution, moving on to evolutionary economics. This study combines his background in econometrics, health economics and evolutionary economics. He lives in Frederick, Maryland, with his wife Kathryn Groth; both husband and wife dote on their toy poodle,

Mark S. Freeland is an economist in the National Health Statistics Group, Office of the Actuary at the federal Centers for Medicare & Medicaid Services in Baltimore, Maryland. He got his Ph.D. at the University of Wisconsin at Madison with emphasis on labor economics and agricultural economics. His research areas include the role of technology in health care cost increases, productivity measurement, price indexes, health care expenditure projections and economic methodology, publishing over 20 articles.

# References

i Peden, E.A., and M.S. Freeland, "Insurance effects on U.S. medical spending (1960-1990)" Health Affairs 1995; 7 and Peden, E.A., and M.S. Freeland, "Insurance effects on U.S. medical spending (1960-1993)" Health Economics 1998; 7.
ii Foster, J., "The self-organizational perspective," in The Evolutionary Foundations of Economics, editor Kurt Dopfer, Cambridge University Press, Cambridge UK: p 383.
iii Kauffman, Stuart A., Reinventing the Sacred, Perseus Book Group, New York, NY, p 120.
iv Beinhocker, Eric D., The Origin of Wealth, Harvard Business School Press, Boston Massachusetts, 2006, p 12. This is an excellent exposition of evolutionary economics.
v Ibid. Beinhocker. p 12.
vi Ibid. Beinhocker. p 13.
vii Ibid. Beinhocker. p 13.
viii Dopfer, Kurt and Jason Potts, The General Theory of Economic Evolution, Routledge, New York, NY: p 6.
xix Ibid. Dopfer and Potts,. pp 6-10.
x Op. Cit. Beinhocker, pp 18 and 19.
xi Page, SE, Understanding Complexity, Course guide from the Teaching Company, Chantilly, VA, 2009.
xii Axelrod, R. and MD Cohen, Harnessing Complexity, Basic Books, New York, 2000.
xiii Blaug, Mark (1998), 'Where are we now in British health economics?', Health Economics, 7: S63-S78. Also found in Hodgson, Geoffrey M., "Towards an alternative economics of health care", Health Economics: Policy and Law, 4: Cambridge University Press, pp 99 and 110.
xiv Ibid. Hodgson, p 100.
xv Dopfer, K, J Foster, and J Potts. "Micro-meso-macro", Journal of Evolutionary Economics, Springer-Verlag (2004) 14: 263-279; p 263.
xvi Ibid. Dopfer, Foster, and Potts: p 263.
xvii Kauffman S, Reinventing the Sacred, Basic Books, New York, 2008, p 176.
xviii Ibid. Kauffman, pp 174-176.
xix "About the Predictability and Complexity of Complex Systems," found in From System Complexity to Emergent Properties, M. A. Aziz-Alaoui and C. Bertelle (Eds.), Springer-Verlag, Berlin Heidelberg, 2009: p 26.

xx. Thomasson, M, "Health Insurance in the United States", Miami University; 2009.
xxi. Personal communication with the author.
xxii. Friedman, M., *Price Theory*, Transaction Publishers, New Brunswick, NJ, 2007: pp 77-82.
xxiii. BEA health consumption data (website: http://www.bea.gov/bea/dn/nipaweb/TableView.asp#Mid) differs slightly from the NHE personal health care spending cited above, which includes a few spending categories not included in BEA data.
xxiv. Thomasson, M., "Health Insurance in the United States", Miami University; 2009. EH.Net Encyclopedia: Health Insurance in the United States.
xxv. Krugman, P., *The Self-Organizing Economy*, Blackwell Publishers, Malden Massachusetts, 1996, p 58 fn.1.
xxvi. Ulanowicz, Robert E., *A Third Window*, Templeton Foundation Press, West Conshohocken, PA, 2009: Chapter 4.
xxvii. BEA website, 2010 (http://www.bea.gov/bea/dn/nipaweb/TableView.asp#Mid).
xxviii. Ibid. Consumption data from the Bureau of Economic Analysis, Commerce Dept., Washington, DC, 2010.
xxix. Consumption data from the Bureau of Economic Analysis, Commerce Dept., Washington, DC, 2010 (website: http://www.bea.gov/bea/dn/nipaweb/TableView.asp#Mid).
xxx. Op. Cit. Bureau of Economic Analysis, Commerce Dept., Washington, DC, 2010.
xxxi. See Newhouse, J, "An Iconoclastic View of Health Cost Containment" *Health Affairs* Supplement 19ed. 93: 159-161.
xxxii. A comprehensive discussion of medical prices is found in *Measuring the Prices of Medical Treatments*, Triplett, Jack E., The Brookings Institution Press, Washington, DC, 2009, particularly the three articles found on pgs. 196–266.
xxxiii. Op. cit. See Foster in Dopfer, *The Evolutionary Foundations of Economics*, p 377.
xxxiv. Ibid. In addition to Foster in Dopfer, p 378, also see Keynes, J. M. (1936), *The General Theory of Employment, Interest and money*, London: Macmillan.
xxxv. Ibid. Foster in Dopfer, p 378.
xxxvi. Op. Cit. Dopfer and Potts, p xii.
xxxvii. Foster, J, and P Wild, "Econometric modeling in the presence of evolutionary change." *Cambridge Journal of Economics* **23**(6), 1999: 749-70.
xxxviii. Op. Cit. Peden and Freeland, 1995, and Peden and Freeland, "Insurance effects on U.S. medical spending (1960-1993)" *Health Economics* 1998; 7: 671-687.

| | |
|---|---|
| xxxix | Dopfer, Kurt and Jason Potts, The General Theory Of Economic Evolution, Routledge, London and New York: 2008. |
| xl | Op. Cit. Foster and Wild. pp 749-770. |
| xli | Op. Cit. Dopfer and Potts, p 11. |
| xlii | Foster, J., "The self-organizing perspective", in Dopfer ed., The Evolutionary Foundations of Economics, 2007, p 377. |
| xliii | Op. Cit. Foster and Wild. p 377. |
| xliv | Op. Cit. Dopfer, Foster, and Potts; p 265. |
| xlv | Quoted in Op. Cit. Hodgson, GM, p 177. |
| xlvi | Ibid. Hodgson, GM, p 262. First sub-quote from Laslo, 1987, p 38. The second from Zeleny, 1987, p 393. |
| xlvii | Ibid. Hodgson, GM, pp 234-267. |
| xlviii | Op. Cit. Beinhocker. |
| xlix | Op. Cit. Dopfer and Potts, p 114. |
| l | Op. Cit. Foster and Wild, p 754. |
| li | Uses National Health Expenditure data (NHE) from Cathy Cowan, The Center for Medicare and Medicaid Services (CMS), Office of the Actuary, 2009. |
| lii | Op. Cit., Foster, J., "The self-organizing perspective", p 383. |
| liii | Op. Cit. Foster and Wild, p 755. |
| liv | Op. Cit. Foster and Wild, p 767. |
| lv | The Center for Medicare and Medicaid Services (CMS), Office of the Actuary, has developed a spending index reflecting health care consumption based on age and gender (2006). |
| lvi | Research spending is from the National Health Accounts (see note xiv). Net domestic product is from the BEA website (see note xx). |
| lvii | Manning, W. G., Newhouse, J.P., Duan, N., Keeler, E.B., Leibowitz, A., and Marquis, M.S., "Health insurance and the demand for medical care: evidence from a randomized experiment". American Economic Review 1987; **77**: 251-277. |
| lviii | The latter is found in the Bureau of Economic Analysis website (http://www.bea.gov/bea/dn/nipaweb/TableView.asp#Mid), 2010. |
| lix | Contact the man who assisted me for details of these studies: <Mark.Freeland@cms.hhs.gov>. |
| lx | Foster J. and P. Wild (1996), Cambridge Journal of Economics **23**(6): pp 749-770. |
| lxi | Op. Cit., BEA website: http://www.bea.gov/bea/dn/nipaweb/TableView.asp#Mid, 2008. |
| lxii | Hartman, Micah B., Robert J. Kornfeld, and Aaron C. Catlin, "A Reconciliation of Health Care Expenditures in the National Health Expenditures Accounts and in Gross Domestic Product," Survey of Current Business 90 (September 2010): 42-52. |
| lxiii | Peden, E.A., and M.S. Freeland, "Insurance Effects on U.S. Medical Spending (1960-1993)" Health Economics 1998; 7: 671-687. |
| lxiv | Op. Cit., Cowan, NHE data, 2009. |

| | |
|---|---|
| lxv | Net domestic product is from the BEA website: http://www.bea.gov/bea/dn/nipaweb/TableView.asp#Mid, 2009. |
| lxvi | Op Cit. Manning, et. al. 1987. |
| lxvii | Finkelstein, A., "The aggregate effects of Health Insurance: Evidence from the Introduction of Medicare", <u>The Quarterly Journal of Economics</u>, Vol. CCXXII, February 2007, Issue 1. |
| lxviii | Garber, Alan M., Charles I. Jones, and Paul M. Romer, <u>Insurance and Incentives for Medical Innovation</u>, NBER Working Paper 12080, National Bureau of Economic Research, Cambridge, MA, 2006: p 24. |
| lxix | Op. Cit. Dopfer and Potts, 2008. |
| lxx | Goodman, J., Health Alert, "Where Are the Innovators in Health Delivery?" See website: john goodman@ncpa.org, National Center for Policy Analysis: Aug 3, 2010. |
| lxxi | For example, see the Huffington Post on the internet for March 15th 2012. |
| lxxii | Nelson, Richard R., *Technology, Institutions and economic growth,* Harvard University Press, Cambridge, Massachusetts, 2005: pp 221-222. |
| lxxiii | Op. Cit. Goodman. |
| lxxiv | See Goodman, John C., and Gerald L. Musgrave, *Patient power: solving America's health care crisis*. Cato Institute, Washington, D.C., 1992. Also John C. Goodman, "Medical Savings Accounts: The Private Sector Already Has Them", National Center for Policy Analysis, Brief Analysis No. 105, April 20, 1994. The more recent form of this idea is Health Savings Accounts (HSAs). John C. Goodman along with Gerald L. Musgrave and Devon M. Herrick have laid out the rationale for and the functioning mechanism for HSAs in John C. Goodman, Gerald L. Musgrave, and Devon M. Herrick, *Lives at Risk (Single-Payer National Health Insurance Around the World)*. Rowan & Littlefield Publishing Group, Inc., Lanham, MD., 2004: Part 3. |
| lxxv | Also see Congressional Research Service report. Washington, D.C. April 2005. |
| lxxvi | See Bosworth, Barry P., <u>Tax Incentives and Economic Growth</u>, The Brookings Institution, Washington, D.C., 1984. pp 142—144. |
| lxxvii | Op. Cit. Nelson, p 226. |
| lxxviii | Ibid. Nelson, p 224. |
| lxxix | Ibid. Nelson, p 224. |
| lxxx | Goodman, John C., <u>Priceless (Curing the Health Care Crisis)</u>, 2012. The Independent Institute, Oakland, California. |

www.ingramcontent.com/pod-product-compliance
Lightning Source LLC
Chambersburg PA
CBHW030915180526
45163CB00004B/1842